Praise for François Sicart and *Luck Is No...*

"François Sicart has given us a riveti... moving and instructive. The book ... a personal story of growth and adaptation in difficult cultural contexts with the evolution of a profound professional worldview.

As a human document, this is an inspiring study of the sensitivities of transcultural life and is full of rare, philosophically rich insights from a long experience in the world of investment—insights that constitute a consummate vision of the global financial landscape.

Luck Is Not Enough is essential reading for both the informed general reader and the more specialized professional."

Ralph Buultjens
Senior professor, New York University
Former Nehru professor, Cambridge University (UK)
Toynbee Prize awardee

"It is incredibly rare to experience the life journey of a *personne de confiance*, a person whose life is given to serving others. In *Luck Is Not Enough*, you will take such a journey with François Sicart as he seeks to help the second, third, and fourth generations of families he has served throughout his lifetime dynamically preserve their families' well-being and their financial resources. You and your family will be well rewarded by the gift of his experience."

James E. Hughes Jr.
Author, *Family: The Compact Among Generations*
Coauthor, *Complete Family Wealth; The Cycle of the Gift; The Voice of the Rising Generation; Family Trusts*

"I remember that my very first thought upon meeting François was wondering how someone could be so physically imposing yet so kind. Over the years of knowing him, I discovered a sharp-minded individual of great humbleness who always showed a real interest in his interlocutors.

Adventurer at heart, he appeared to me as someone who naturally thought outside the box. His curiosity, as well as his attraction to novelty and opportunities, made him stand out of the crowd.

In *Luck Is Not Enough*, François recognizes not only that he was lucky, but that he knew he had to take this chance, this chance that we sometimes don't see until it appears.

From Tucker Anthony to Tocqueville Asset Management, then to Sicart Associates, François became a successful asset manager, family office, and homme d'affaires (an elegant set of words he used in his book and that I had not read for decades in my French native language!).

I remember when François first explained to me his contrarian philosophy regarding financial investments. Initially amazed, I became deeply interested by the originality of his strategy, which greatly differed from the secure classical benchmarked approach used by the majority of asset managers of the time.

Despite his strong gut feeling, François would not rush investment decisions before understanding their implications. Would he have an interest for investing in a company based in China? He would simply book a flight and travel all the way there to be sure of his decision.

As François writes: 'The world is full of treasures hidden in plain sight.' For someone like me, taking my chance was to build, with trust and serenity, a very special friendship with him."

Bruno Julien-Laferrière
Executive chairman, Banque Transatlantique

FRANÇOIS SICART

LUCK

IS

NOT ENOUGH

THE LIFE AND LEGACY OF A

SUCCESSFUL WEALTH MANAGER

Published by Advantage, Charleston, South Carolina.
Member of Advantage Media Group.

ADVANTAGE is a registered trademark, and the Advantage colophon is a trademark of Advantage Media Group, Inc.

Printed in the United States of America.

10 9 8 7 6 5 4 3 2 1

ISBN: 978-1-64225-169-2
LCCN: 2021916007

Cover design by George Stevens.
Layout design by Wesley Strickland.

This publication is designed to provide accurate and authoritative information in regard to the subject matter covered. It is sold with the understanding that the publisher is not engaged in rendering legal, accounting, or other professional services. If legal advice or other expert assistance is required, the services of a competent professional person should be sought.

Advantage Media Group is proud to be a part of the Tree Neutral® program. Tree Neutral offsets the number of trees consumed in the production and printing of this book by taking proactive steps such as planting trees in direct proportion to the number of trees used to print books. To learn more about Tree Neutral, please visit **www.treeneutral.com**.

Advantage Media Group is a publisher of business, self-improvement, and professional development books and online learning. We help entrepreneurs, business leaders, and professionals share their Stories, Passion, and Knowledge to help others Learn & Grow. Do you have a manuscript or book idea that you would like us to consider for publishing? Please visit **advantagefamily.com**.

To the wonderful women who have guided and protected my journey. First and foremost my wife Régine, but also Lucille, Marcella, Genevieve, Patsy, and Delphine.

And to my two children, Daniel and Laureen, who may have suffered in the early years from my busy schedule and frequent travel but still managed to turn out well and to constitute, with Régine and me, a smoothly functioning family.

Contents

Acknowledgments

THERE ARE MANY people who have graciously expressed their support of me and of this book. In addition, of course, to my wife, Régine, these include:

Lucille Galgano, who was the indispensable assistant to Tucker Anthony's senior partner when I joined the firm as an ignorant new analyst. Lucille was often overworked and stressed but nevertheless always took time to teach me how to write tickets, process orders, and do other basic tasks of this new business.

Marcella Lang worked with me for about thirty-seven years. She was my main conduit to the rest of the firms, aware of everything about both clients and employees but always a model of discretion.

Of course, my now partner, **Patsy Jaganath**, who is presented at greater length within the book.

Delphine Chevalier, who is the warm and welcoming voice of my office in Paris and who efficiently and cheerfully guides me through the complexities of French bureaucracy and other local aggravations. Problems always seem to shrink when she gets involved.

Diandra Ramsammy, a more recent addition to Sicart Associates, a jack-of-all-trades adept in answering the queries and solving the problems of the firm's four partners, always with a smile.

China was a milestone of my career ever since I visited it for the first time, during the Asian crisis of 1997. It started with a small group of young French entrepreneurs, who not only helped with the language but invaluably served as translators of the culture for me. Among them, **Alain Savouré**, **Yann Lombard-Platet** and **Jérôme Lacrosnière**, who all created enterprises in China during the "frontier" days. Ultimately, they were joined by **Zhen Qi Nan**, **Zhen Xiangsha** and **Li Ming**, **Peter Q. Pan**, and **Xu Xiaonian**, who introduced me to the strength and durability of Chinese friendship.

I met **Ralph Buultjens** when we were both invited at the same time to speak at the International Study and Research Institute. A casual conversation then evolved into a long friendship with this highly unusual thinker, whose firsthand experience of many cultures is supplemented by a profound knowledge of history. Ralph was a professor at both New York University and Cambridge University and lectured at several other prestigious venues. He also has been policy advisor to several international leaders, and both Prime Ministers Indira Gandhi and Sirimavo Bandaranaike have written introductions to his own books.

Jay Hugues was, before he retired, a lawyer famous for helping complex and sometimes dysfunctional families communicate despite differences and generation gaps. I met him when I was challenged to try and create some consensus among six children who had just inherited from a headstrong father who had been my client. They would not even speak to each other, but when the daughter put me in contact with Jay, it marked the beginning of an education of what it means to construct and protect a family wealth over several generations. Jay continues to graciously advise me and now my younger partners.

I resigned from the board of directors of Banque Transatlantique practically within days of **Bruno Julien-Laferrière** being elected CEO of that institution, and I felt obligated to invite him to lunch to explain that my resignation had nothing to do with him but was, in fact, due to irreconcilable scheduling conflicts between my travels and the bank's board meetings. At the time, the bank was known primarily as the institution serving members of the French diplomatic corps—a clientele not particularly wealthy but quite demanding and located around the world.

Under Bruno's leadership, the bank grew and became one of the few *truly* private banks remaining in France. I was particularly impressed by his style of management, maintaining and enhancing the house's culture of personalized service while taking full advantage of a rare ability to delegate responsibilities and empower his staff.

Finally, I would like to thank Carol and David, who respectively edited my regular articles and this book and managed to make my English look more eloquent and friendly than how it naturally comes out.

A Fortunate Journey

SOME PEOPLE BELIEVE that fate, God, the universe, or some other unseen force predetermines our destiny. We just show up on time and hope the ticket we've been given in the cosmic lottery is a winner.

Others contend that fate or luck have little to do with the outcome of our life, that everything springs from the individual will, which is the sole determinant of whether and how we make the most of our time on earth. Attributing one's success or failure to random factors like luck is, they say, just an excuse, or even a fallacy.

My belief lies somewhere in the middle: we all have agency to choose freely, and at any given moment, we exercise the capacity to pursue this path or that one, go through this door or that one—an infinitude of possibilities. But luck also plays a role in shaping our life, like a mysterious light that turns on periodically in a dark forest: illuminating a different path, giving us the option to take it or not.

The kind of luck that interests me isn't just random; it's more than a coin flip. It means understanding that inevitably, good things happen by chance, entirely out of your control, often impossible to predict, but when they do, it's up to you to recognize the opportunity and make the most of it.

I think that we all have some luck, but often we don't see the opportunities when they appear. The savvy individual—and the savvy investor—has his eyes and ears attuned to the manifold signals the world is throwing out. Some opportunities announce themselves gently, like a whisper in the night, so quiet that it's hard to tell if it was a voice or merely the wind. Other opportunities might call out to you loudly, blaring and flashing like a fire alarm, but they're as ephemeral as they are conspicuous: blink, and they'll be gone forever.

As I've learned in my nearly fifty-year-long journey in finance, even smart, successful people routinely fail to spot opportunities that are staring them in the face. In large part because of my capacity to recognize these opportunities, I've thrived as an investor and money manager for many important families.

Often the best opportunities are found in the least likely places, and that mindset forms the basis of the contrarian investment philosophy that has served me well over several generations of building wealth for individuals and families in the United States and abroad.

In many ways, my whole career has been a happy accident. I started in accounting before completing compulsory military service in France, the country of my birth, and then a few twists of fate led me to New York and Wall Street. I founded Tocqueville Asset Management at the age of thirty, a small company of just five people. By 2016, it had grown into a one-hundred-and-thirty-person firm with over $13 billion in assets under management.

That same year, looking for a change and a new challenge, I recruited three of my top colleagues at Tocqueville, and together we founded a new venture, Sicart Associates, where I remain today. This book is, in many ways, as much about my three colleagues as it is about me, for though we represent different generations and hail from different backgrounds, our careers have been intimately intertwined, and they've been essential in developing Sicart Associates into a boutique powerhouse in just a few short years.

One of the reasons I founded Sicart Associates was because I wanted to captain a company that went beyond the purview of typical wealth management firms and could serve as an homme d'affaires for our clients. Traditionally, an homme d'affaires is a trusted advisor that has a close relationship with his clients and is versed not just in matters of the purse but is also knowledgeable in other vital professions, such as law and accounting. We don't merely handle our clients' portfolios; we also interface with attorneys, tax experts, accountants, and trustees, which we believe is essential to preserving our clients' fortunes (in both senses of the word).

In this way, we can fulfill the complex interdisciplinary demands of twenty-first-century patrimony management, much like the homme d'affaires of the past, whose counsel served aristocrats, nobles, merchants, and other luminaries across multiple generations. *Luck Is Not Enough* reflects my long-held belief that families who are building and maintaining a patrimony need a generalist who understands the big picture of family dynamics in addition to being a skilled investor and expert steward of capital.

> **Money management isn't only about investing; it is about relationships, facilitating connections, and making a promise to future generations.**

Families and finances are perhaps some of the most complicated aspects of our lives. Places where these factors intersect are personal, emotional, and intense, carrying the weight of past experiences and future expectations. Money management isn't only about investing; it is about relationships, facilitating connections, and making a promise to future generations.

This book is decades in the making, a compendium of everything I've learned over the last half century, a chronicle of my triumphs and trip-ups, of bubbles and crashes, of the moguls and mavens and mentors (some long since departed from this world) who taught me well, and whose own talent and perspicacity live on in me and my firm (and now in this book).

I hope that you find the stories that follow entertaining as well as edifying, for I want to share with you not only the story of my life, but the wisdom about investment that can guide your own philosophy of saving, investing, and living.

PART 1

An Opportunity and An Education

CHAPTER 1

The Snowstorm That Changed My Fate

Killington, Vermont, 1969

THE WIND WHIPPED down from the mountaintop and across the snowy, undulating slopes with the force of a thousand Roman chariots rushing into battle, its icy chill as sharp as the tip of a spear. The snow had started falling in the morning and hadn't let up, as my American cousin, his wife, and I sipped after-dinner cocktails in the wood-paneled warmth of the ski lodge. A full-on blizzard with no sign of abating. Normally, that might have been a welcome development during a ski holiday—at the very least, we could have whiled away the hours in the comfort of the lodge—but I had a couple of important appointments awaiting me back in New York. I had traveled from Paris for two weeks to find work, a narrow window in which my whole future was at stake. But Mother Nature was conspiring to keep me away.

"What are the chances of this clearing?" I asked my cousin. He knew I had an interview on Monday afternoon.

He smiled with pity. "Don't get your hopes up, François. Just look outside. Three feet of snow already, with another four on the way, and more of the same is happening in New York."

"And how much is a foot?" I asked. I had only been in the States for a few days at that point. The imperial system of measurement was, like decaffeinated coffee, nondairy creamer, sugarless sweetener, and other uniquely American things, new to me.

It had taken months of networking, letter writing, and long-distance phone calls to finagle the interviews, not to mention the time and expense of transatlantic travel (which was a much greater undertaking back then). As I watched the snow continue to fall, I accepted that my cousin's forecast was probably the right one: we weren't getting out of Vermont any time soon.

At the first opportunity, I called the man I was supposed to meet with in New York. He was apologetic, but he refused to reschedule; they had other candidates to interview. It does not leave a good impression on a prospective employer when you miss the interview because you had gone north to ski for the weekend, force majeure notwithstanding. The other meetings I had set up dissolved, too, like melting snow.

What then? I was never one to despair or lose my cool, and I've always thrived on challenges, but the situation seemed dire.

I was about to learn an important lesson that has stayed with me ever since.

The Man in the Gray Cashmere Suit
Paris, 1969

What I remember most about La Gaudriole was its bistro-like interior, its original 360-degree mural depicting the famous Longchamp horse races of the nineteenth century, and the perpetual state of barely contained chaos and the pleasant clatter that prevailed inside that little restaurant: drinks prepared, orders taken, food plated, money exchanged, counted, and secured away with the constant and jovial intrusion of the owner into each table's conversation. And of course, the overlap of a dozen voices, mingling and mixing.

The restaurant was nestled on a busy street in the first arrondissement, with a window on the gardens of the Palais Royal, close to the Louvre. My then-girlfriend Régine and I ate lunch there almost every day. That day seemed like any other day, but through a simple twist of fate, it would prove to be one of the most pivotal meals of my life.

We were dining with a few friends, young Parisians like us, trying to make their way in the world, when the subject of my career plans came up.

"Have you told them yet?" Régine said. Régine had thick black hair with bangs and dark eyes—an alluring Cleopatra look. She was always dressed in very fashionable clothes, even though she worked all day in her atelier.

"Tell us what?" said Antoine, a journalist friend of ours.

"Some exciting news," said Régine, her eyes lighting up as they always did at the thought of a fresh challenge, a new adventure.

"You're finally being court-martialed?" our friend joked.

"Not yet, though there's still time for that," I said. "No, but seriously: you know I'm visiting my cousin in America next week. I'm going to look for work there. Régine and I are, if all goes well, moving to New York."

"New York!" he said. "What's wrong with Paris?"

"Nothing's wrong with Paris. We love Paris. But there are opportunities there that you can't find here."

Our friend whistled and shook his head, but his grin told me he approved.

"He's right, actually," said the man at the next table. A young-looking forty-something Italian man, he wore a perfectly tailored gray cashmere suit. I had never seen him before, but at La Gaudriole, most of the clientele were regulars (many writers and journalists), and the tables were packed tightly, so it was common, expected even, to banter with other patrons.

"New York abounds with opportunity. Full steam ahead there. Paris is a museum, old, beautiful, and elegant. New York is a locomotive, dynamic, fast, noisy, and dirty. I just returned from there myself," the Italian said. "What do you intend to do there?"

"Wall Street," I answered. Two words that everyone in the world recognizes immediately. Two words that convey prestige, ambition, affluence, and risk.

"Interesting. Cutthroat. But that's where the money is made. Myself, I'm in publishing. Don't know much about finance. But a good friend of mine works for Tucker Anthony, the brokerage. He's very busy and may not have any time for you. But look him up if you're in New York. Tell him Ranieri Sanminiatelli says hello."

"Thanks," I said, not thinking much of it, not even bothering to write down the name. There were eight million people in New York. I didn't think any of them would want to arrange a meeting with me out of the blue. Besides, at that point I already had a few appointments lined up via contacts from the alumni of my business school.

"Good luck, my friend," said Ranieri, who polished off his coffee, put on his hat, and left. I never saw him again. Nor did I know (nor he, for that matter) that he just inadvertently changed my life.

At the time, I hadn't really begun a career. A few experiments had given me a taste of one field or another, but nothing seduced me. I had completed an MBA at the leading French business school, after which I taught accounting for two years—ironic, because I was actually a very poor student in accounting. But no one else applied for the job, and under the tutelage of two American professors, I became proficient enough to teach others, even though my students—candidates for the French equivalent of certified public accountant—probably had a better grasp of the subject than me. (I saved face by teaching the "philosophy" of accounting.)

After teaching, I fulfilled my compulsory military service with the air force, but during peacetime, there wasn't much for servicemen to do. I didn't even see a single plane during my two-month basic training. The air force really recruited me for its volleyball team at the air ministry in Paris, which was probably the best way one can spend a period of conscription.

As I neared the end of my stint in the military, I still had no idea of what I really wanted to do. I had some interest in biology and toyed with the idea of going into business, but finance was not on the radar until my friend Joel Maunoury suggested that I work on Wall Street.

Joel and his wife Dominique (Dodo) were between us and our parents in age, a couple whom we admired as the paragon of good taste. He'd had a career as an executive in a large industrial company and then as a banker. Régine and I had assumed that Dominique was a housewife until we were invited to celebrate her retirement with them: she had been an executive VP of a major insurance company without ever mentioning it.

"Do you like money?" Joel asked me one day.

"I certainly don't mind it," I said. And so the idea was born.

I gave it some thought and talked it over with Régine. It was not an easy decision because, among other reasons, she had a child from a previous marriage (whom we were raising as our own). But she was also enthusiastic about the plan, understanding the opportunity that awaited me on the other side of the ocean. We both decided New York was where our future lay, maybe not for a lifetime, but at least for a couple years. We were both young, at that age when one feels one can do anything, when time is limitless and the world is full of promise.

And so, one by one, the stars began to align.

When One Door Closes ...

Stars. So many of them in the Vermont sky in that era. Decades of development and light pollution have dimmed their dazzle somewhat. But back then, Vermont was, even more than today, a rural appendage hanging off the northeast tip of the United States, a borderland of regal granite mountains, white snowy hills, and pristine evergreen forest—and a bright, crystalline, star-studded sky, more than I had ever seen, certainly more than you'd see in Paris today.

I stood there, marveling at the heavens, wondering what would come next. I was running out of time.

My cousins and I took the train back to New York two days later. I had three days before my flight back to Paris, but I was determined not to return empty-handed. As I pondered my options, I remembered the Italian publisher in La Gaudriole; I racked my brain to recall the name of his friend, which I had not bothered to write down. Like a starburst, it popped into my mind: Giorgio Uzielli.

This was, of course, the era when if you wanted someone's phone number, you looked them up in the phone book. In a city of millions, there was only one Giorgio Uzielli listed. I dialed and waited with bated breath, hoping the number still belonged to Giorgio and not, say, an old European tailor or a Chinese delivery restaurant.

It may be a cliché to talk about "the one phone call that changed your life," but that was mine. Giorgio picked up, and I told him who I was and how I got his number. Since both he and Ranieri were from Florence, he felt he had to be nice.

"I'd love to see you," he said, "but I'm going to Europe tonight. Can you meet now? We can have a quick chat."

I met him in his office, a place where (little did I know it) I would spend many of my waking hours over the next few years of my life. Tucker Anthony had twin headquarters in Boston and New York (with an office at 120 Broadway, in the heart of the Financial District).

We spoke for an hour or so, in which time Giorgio told me there was another Frenchman there, a youngish man who recently made senior partner, so he introduced us. That was my first meeting with Christian Humann, a man who would become a lifelong mentor, friend, and confidante, and who would shape my life in many ways. (Surely this book would not exist without him.)

Christian and I had a long, interesting talk, and he queried me about my background, interests, and professional history. I suppose it was an impromptu job interview, but it was really more of a friendly conversation. I didn't feel pressured to "perform" or to present myself in any particular way.

After an hour, Christian said, "I like you, François, and I think you'd do well here. But we don't have an open position now. In fact, we don't even have a desk for you."

"Thank you anyway," I said. "If things change … "

"Well, wait a minute. Let me call our office in Boston. Boston isn't New York. It's certainly not Paris. But it's a charming city and a prestigious financial center, and there are some excellent people who work for us there. I'll see what I can do. Let's meet tomorrow for lunch at The Bankers Club. It happens to be in this building."

Meanwhile, Régine's mother recoiled at the thought of her daughter running off with a man who was, in her eyes, basically just a student. So she had her own misgivings about our plans.

I suppose this disapproval of her mother and my parents became a source of bonding between them, because in the months after Régine and I departed for New York, they became quite good friends. It was a rocky period of familial relations that took some time to overcome; there was some stubbornness on both sides, and a long time during which Régine and I spoke infrequently with our family back home, a rift that was certainly not helped by the communication barriers inherent to transatlantic living—in those days before Skype and email, the only real link between the continents was a telephone cable at the bottom of the ocean.

Eventually, Régine and I got married, on my lunch hour and at city hall, since we didn't know yet that you could hire your own justice of the peace. My cousin, who was extremely supportive throughout these early years, even translated into English some of our official French papers. Still, I'm happy to say that the birth of our daughter some time after that brought an end to the family discord as if it had never happened.

But in those first few months in New York, the challenges were immense, and not just because of family issues. It was a new country, new culture, new career, new life. The moment our plane touched down in New York, the familiar was replaced with the unfamiliar. The old was swept out by the new. But that is really the spirit of New York, a metropolis that is always rushing ahead, remaking and reimagining itself, tearing down and building back up, powered by the creativity and energy of its residents. An obsession with novelty and progress that is reflected in the myriad young people who leave their hometowns for New York in search of success. And so it was for us, too.

We knew it would be a struggle. But we had the confidence to face it.

The Lesson: Spot and Seize Opportunities

Investors must be alert to opportunities, which are more often covert than they are overt. In an efficient market, everyone is competing for the slightest edge; everybody is racing to get on board today with tomorrow's winner. Once an asset or company is "discovered," the price shoots up. It's hard to excel in this business if you're always late to the party.

If you want to beat your competitors to the punch, you have to be among the first to recognize emergent opportunities. When

> **Recognizing opportunity is not merely a business skill; it's a certain attitude toward life.**

everyone is looking left, you should be looking right. That's the essence of being a contrarian investor, a strategy that I've followed throughout my career and which guides our decisions at Sicart Associates.

Recognizing opportunity is not merely a business skill; it's a certain attitude toward life. Most people move from day to day with their eyes fixed firmly in front of them, missing what is happening at the periphery, which is precisely where the best opportunities lie. You have to attune your vision and change your whole mindset, recognizing when a good thing comes your way while perfecting your analysis of its potential risk and reward.

It's not just about having the right information either. Today, even the casual investor buying or selling a few shares of Tesla with his brokerage account has more financial and economic data available than Wall Street professionals had even twenty years ago (and certainly more than I had as a young analyst in the late '60s and early '70s). But that abundance of information is both a blessing and a curse: information overload only makes it harder to separate the signal from the noise.

> **Luck is not just a passive state of hoping things will turn out for the best, but an active cultivation of readiness to seize upon opportunity when it emerges.**

You have to see what you can't see. Cultivate a sixth sense. To be successful in investing, luck is essential, and I have had my fair share of it. You can't really forecast the future, but you can prepare, recognize, and seize the opportunity.

Luck is not just a passive state of hoping things will turn out for the best, but an active cultivation of readiness to seize upon opportunity when it emerges.

The world is full of treasure hidden in plain sight. A man buys a cheap landscape painting at a flea market and later discovers a priceless, original copy of the Declaration of Independence hidden behind the frame. A working-class Scotsman tending to an industrial estate stumbles upon a marble bust propping open a shed door and finds out that doorstop is an eighteenth-century work of art that later sells for $2 million at auction. These are both true stories, and they have a lot to teach us. These are extraordinary occurrences, but you need not depend on a once-in-a-lifetime stroke of luck to succeed. Just optimize the luck you are given and make the most of it.

Look where others aren't looking, for there you will find the source of untold riches that will change your life.

hired to fulfill a specific need or fill an open position. Yet I knew that as long as there was a space for me, I could prove my worth.

As a senior partner, Christian was very busy and had little time to talk to me, but when the work day ended, I would join him in his corner office, and there we would have long, stimulating talks, during which he would teach me the ins and outs of the business, and I would bounce questions off him and process what I had learned and experienced that day. These informal, after-hours lessons were an invaluable source of my education in the field.

Christian was an exceptional man, and not only because he excelled at his job. He was highly educated and was well-read in French, American, and English literature. He had a passion for opera and art, particularly Indian art, several pieces of which adorned his office and would eventually be displayed by the Asia Society and various other museums.

He enjoyed sourcing hard-to-find art pieces, which in some respects reflected his investing strategy, as he had a knack for finding opportunities that were totally out of favor but would later bloom in value. In spite of my ignorance of the art world, his tutelage was formative in developing the contrarian philosophy that has enabled me to build not one but two thriving wealth management companies.

Investment banking was a different beast back then. There were no Bloomberg terminals or algorithmic high-frequency trading pumping out dozens of orders per second. It was still, in many ways, a human-oriented, face-to-face business, relatively low-tech, and dependent on raw brain power and investigative zeal to succeed.

Automation, digitization, and the proliferation of data has revolutionized the industry in a way few of us would have anticipated in the early 1970s. But what the professional traders and investors working on Wall Street lacked in information abundance they made up for in their assiduous study of companies and markets.

And there was a galaxy of knowledge in the heads of the fifteen partners and fifty or sixty brokers at Tucker Anthony's New York office: old-school analysts, traders, and financial wizards who knew the companies they were buying inside out. Many of them specialized in one sector or industry: railroads, banks, mining, chemicals—the constituent elements of America's great postwar economic engine.

Today, brokers are so consumed by selling a panoply of products designed by marketing departments and mathematicians that they don't really know how to analyze companies anymore. But these men (and in those days, brokers were almost exclusively men) would pore over annual reports, talk to management, seek out data wherever they could find it. Information was harder to come by than it is today— you had to dig deep. Every financial fact, figure, or footnote you could unearth first gave you a competitive advantage.

This was the atmosphere in which I began my tenure. My first days at Tucker Anthony were a whirlwind of education. They broke me in quickly, and I learned a great deal in a short period of time. I benefited from incredible mentorship during those years, and after decades in the business, I've come full circle, acting as a mentor to the younger professionals in my employ (who will eventually continue the cycle when they take on protégés of their own). To this day I remain grateful for their guidance.

The Three Musketeers

In the beginning, as I said, I had no official title—I was a broker, basically, but I was doing a lot of things at once. Much of my day-to-day work revolved around assisting three important individuals who had once been Christian's early partners and were now our clients. These three men also became important mentors to me.

Now in their seventies, they had all been in the business since before the Great Depression, and the hard lessons of that terrible period helped mold them into shrewd investors. They came from unique backgrounds and had different strengths, so their distinct skillsets complemented each other and made for ideal on-the-job training for a neophyte like myself.

I worked most closely with Walter Mewing. His success was particularly impressive because he was self-taught and self-made—he did not have a university degree in a milieu where most of the men who rose to senior partner came from blue-blooded stock and had relied on family money to kick off their careers.

Walter cut his teeth on Wall Street as a runner in the 1920s, and as he raced around Manhattan delivering messages and documents, learning and observing carefully, he reached a point where he was ready to start putting his own capital into the game. It wasn't much, but in the boom of the Roaring Twenties, it grew into a small fortune—until he decided equities had become too expensive, and he cashed out in 1928. I need not tell you what happened to the market the following year.

Walter withdrew from Wall Street entirely for several years, living a quiet life in the country operating a chicken farm he purchased with his earnings. It wasn't until after the Great Depression that he returned to finance, where he picked up where he left off and eventually multiplied his net worth several times over: the messenger boy turned modest magnate.

Walter was a fantastic analyst with a voracious appetite for information. Each day he attended the meeting of the New York Society of Security Analysts, where he would hobnob with representatives of various companies, gaining valuable insight he could parlay into the next smart investment.

As a disciple of Benjamin Graham, often called the father of value investing, Walter diligently studied companies' data to find underpriced stocks. One of his favorite techniques from Graham, which I incorporated into my

The essential kernel of truth, I learned, is rarely located where it is most obvious, convenient, or accessible. You often must sift through the fine print to find it.

own practice, was to read companies' annual reports starting with the footnotes at the end. The main text of the reports was useful, but it was also loaded with verbiage designed to shape a certain narrative. The oft-ignored footnotes, however, were a goldmine of SEC-mandated disclosures that would give you a more honest, nuanced assessment of a company's finances. That's where you'd pick up on any problems a firm had and the methods they used to calculate their earnings. The essential kernel of truth, I learned, is rarely located where it is most obvious, convenient, or accessible. You often must sift through the fine print to find it.

So Walter took me under his wing and was eager to explain the ins and outs of the business, how to read and interpret annual reports, which questions to ask of management. And we had a little game where I would present to him a company that might be cheap, and he would fire off questions about it to test the depth of my research and the integrity of my conclusion. And that's how I learned how to ask the right questions of management, which I then went and asked.

Of Christian and his former partners I worked alongside, Walter was the investigative man. Christian and the other two would come to him with their ideas, and he would use his analytical chops to evaluate them.

Then there was Joe D'Assern, a man you might say, if you're familiar with Dumas's famous novel, was the Porthos of the group—portly and jovial and full of life. He would often bring flowers to the secretaries in the office, and he had a bottomless supply of jokes and one-liners that he would deploy with the skillful timing of a standup comic.

But Joe could also be intimidating. In the early years of our relationship, he just refused to speak to me. He would call on our direct line to speak to Christian and, if he was away in Europe or Asia and I offered to help, he would answer, "No, thank you. I will call when he returns." Later, he would call only to ask if I thought the reported earnings of a company were accurate and the balance sheet was clean, but never to ask my opinion about an investment. Only much later would we discuss the desirability of investment. But he always decided to buy or sell and at what price.

On another occasion, I remember one day I showed up to the office in a plaid suit, very fashionable at the time. It was the first suit I bought in America, and I wore it with pride. Another broker took one look at me and said, "Going to the races?" Joe laughed along with the rest of the brokers. Evidently it wasn't formal enough for that environment.

Joe was an audacious, fearless investor who had a great penchant for holding fast during a protracted drawdown. He would call me and say, "GM is down fifty percent. What do you think of their finances?"

And I'd look at the numbers and tell him, "The balance sheet looks fine; I see nothing wrong."

Then he would start buying aggressively, all the way to the ultimate bottom, without ever blinking. It takes a lot of nerve to do that if it's your own money at stake but *especially*, as I later learned, if you're fielding panicked calls from clients who are begging you to sell.

What I learned from Joe is that once you have checked your ideas, you can be stubborn against the crowd of investors and stick to your guns. In investing, character can be more important than brains or intuition. What Joe taught me is the necessity of courage, provided it's a rational kind of courage and not just blind hope.

That was my first exposure to a truly bold style of contrarian investing, and Joe was living proof that if you know how (or when) to pick a winner and have the steely reserve to hold on, you can get rich from it.

Finally, Bayard Walker, a man whose background was as aristocratic as his name, tall, gray haired, and impeccably polite, was the third former-partner-turned-client Christian paired me with. Bayard came from a prominent background (I believe he was somehow connected to the Lehman family) and counted the Rockefellers among his venture investment associates.

His fortune was concentrated in real estate and oil, and when I met him, he had expanded into venture capital, which was not really my area, and so we didn't work together closely at first, but he taught me many things nonetheless. Later in my career, we collaborated more frequently, and he would seek out my insight into the markets and the economy in general.

Bayard was interesting because his approach was totally different—more akin to the Phil Fisher school of growth investing. He would pay close attention to the management of the companies he was looking at, investing not just in companies but in the people leading them.

Getting Acclimated

Initially, as I said, I didn't have an official title. My day-to-day work chiefly involved researching promising investment opportunities, which I would then take to Christian and the other partners.

My first big report was about American Metal Climax Inc. (AMX), later known as Amax. They were a mining company that was involved in lucrative molybdenum extraction, among other things. I analyzed their company in great detail, putting to use some of the techniques I had learned from my mentors, such as speaking directly with the management.

Fortunately, for some reason, the controller of AMX had taken a liking to me, and his openness made my work easier.

Controllers oversee accounting activities, financial reporting, and budgets but are not considered among a corporation's top executives. For this reason, they are less courted by analysts than CEOs or CFOs. Yet they are pivotal and perhaps the best informed about how the reported profits are arrived at. Mr. Crowl, if I remember his name correctly, told me everything I wanted to know; not that he was giving me any inside information, but he explained where AMX's earnings were generated and how this was reflected in the company's reports.

It seems almost quaint now to think that so much of the research process could be explained by one person over countless hours. In that period, you could get a company's CFO or president on the phone, and they would speak to you freely. Today, they'll just read from a preapproved script vetted by the company's lawyers, if they pick up the phone at all. And it doesn't matter anyway, because anything a senior executive will tell you is already out in the open, for instantaneous consumption, given the speed at which information circulates in the digital era. And, as a rule, you won't have access to people in the lower echelons of the corporation who haven't been briefed by the legal staff about what to say and not say.

Anyway, after several weeks digesting AMX's annual reports and conversing with the controller, I knew about as much as could be known about the firm. In fact, when the company's properties in Zambia were nationalized, I knew instantly how many kwachas it would cost the firm and what the kwacha was worth in US dollars. So I wrote a long report about the stock. But when I presented the idea to some of our partners, they retorted that the company's management had a mediocre reputation. The report was circulated internally but never published for outside clients.

Well, in the following year, the price of metals started rising dramatically. The company was thriving, and the chairman/CEO, Ian McGregor, was suddenly touted as one of the best managers of the year. Now everyone wanted in. Warren Buffett famously said: "When a manager with a reputation for brilliance tackles a business with a reputation for bad economics, the reputation of the business remains intact." The opposite is also true: a change in the fundamentals of an industry (especially a cyclical one) can change investors' perceptions of a management's quality.

I don't know if the senior partners ever gave me credit for having pitched this company at an opportune time, but the important thing was that I learned a lesson for my own career in investing: while management can make or break a company, sometimes even the smartest people in the room are misguided about the quality of that management. In the end, it is the data and the leader's character—not necessarily his recent achievements—that count.

Another early learning experience came when I looked into Chromalloy American, a firm that provided specialized coatings for planes, long-distance diagnosis for doctors, aerospace technology, all kinds of cutting-edge ventures, apparently financed by the cash-cow aerospace activities. I did my research and presented the company to Walter Mewing, but he shot it down right away.

"This company's no good," he said.

"Why not?"

"The management, for one. I don't trust 'em," he said, using a much less politically correct phrasing.

> **You must always judge opinions by the character of the person who proffers them and check the data by yourself.**

I thought Walter's reasons were not convincing, if not downright offensive. So I bought the stock for some client accounts, but it kept disappointing me. Later I found out that although the core aerospace business was solid, they were overextended into too many industries, which made them less profitable, and worse, the narrative surrounding the new ventures changed from one contact to the next. Walter's instinct was right, but it was really based on less prejudiced reasons, and his brief response should have triggered some deeper investigation.

Other people's opinions can be questionable, but they are not always worthless as a result. You must always judge opinions by the character of the person who proffers them and check the data by yourself.

* * *

During my early years, I did not only learn some valuable investment lessons. I also learned about the ethics and principles of running a respectable business. One of these lessons came in our dealings with a major coffee chain company. We were managing their pension fund with the assistance of Walter. This company was close to finalizing a merger with a larger company when Walter brought to our attention that the pension fund that we were managing was grossly overfunded and that there was a real risk that the acquirer could "raid" the pension fund to finance the acquisition.

On his advice, we proposed that the company liquidate the pension fund and use the proceeds to buy annuities for each one of the fund's beneficiaries. The company's CEO readily accepted "because it was the right thing to do for his loyal employees." It was not, however, advantageous for the acquiring company. At the time, this pension fund was an important client for us, which we lost as a result of our suggestion, despite the fact that the CEO was on board.

But there is a moral to that story. Years later, the CEO had passed away, leaving in his estate some oil royalties inherited from his father that, at the then-current oil prices, generated almost no income and were therefore essentially worthless. We held on to them, along with his personal portfolio, which was then relatively modest. But as the years went by and oil prices rose significantly, the royalties began paying income every year. The former CEO's widow ordered them to be paid into her account with us, which allowed her to start planning the disposition of her estate among her children. For many years (until her death) this again became one of our large accounts.

So by doing the right thing, we lost an account, but eventually a larger account came back to us. This reinforced for me the conviction that if you do the right thing, you eventually get rewarded for it, in one form or another. This was, in fact, a lesson my father had always taught me, but now I was seeing how big the reward could be.

CHAPTER 3

An Unfortunate Inheritance

IN THE PARTNERSHIP that Christian and I maintained within the firm, he had the lion's share of the clients, which of course was logical, as he had, over many years, established a strong foundation of trust with these people, most of whom I didn't know well or at all.

And in truth, I wasn't so interested in the interpersonal, client-facing side of things. Rather, I was enthralled by the business itself. I was driven by a desire to perform well and do well by our clients, but I had little interest in really forming a relationship with the people whose capital we managed.

In this respect, Christian and I made an excellent team, since our strengths complemented each other well. I was taking the lead on managing clients' portfolios while Christian was the public face, the guy with whom they cultivated a relationship. But I would soon learn that client relations are not something you can shirk, no matter how strong your performance is. You can't really separate the person from their portfolio.

After I made partner, Christian wanted me to get to know some of our clients better. One particularly headstrong lady gave me a memorable early lesson in the value of trust. She was the heiress of a sewing machine company owned by an aristocratic French-American family. Christian had been managing her accounts for a while, and he arranged for the three of us to have coffee at her home. The plan was that, after talking for a while, Christian would politely excuse himself, giving me and her a chance to get acquainted.

After Christian left and we moved past a bit of initial "blind date" awkwardness, she and I had a pleasant chat for an hour. I left her thinking that it had gone quite well.

The next morning Christian intercepted me on the way to my office. He reported her comment: "I don't care if he's a genius! He's too young, and I don't want him touching my money!'"

Though I was flattered by the implicit compliment, I was a bit discouraged by the outcome. It was suddenly apparent to me that just having "partner" in my title wasn't by itself sufficient to persuade others that I was on equal footing with the senior members of the firm.

Eventually I did assume management of her family's portfolios and in time became a friend of her son and, in turn, his sons, but I would never really deal with her directly. I suppose her mind was made up that I was too green. She passed away long ago, but I would hope that, now that I'm in my seventies, she would find me adequately experienced for the job.

A similar incident happened one or two other times, when Christian would delegate to me the management of a long-standing client's account while having to talk through the client's reservations about working with a partner who hadn't even yet turned thirty.

"But haven't they seen the returns for that account?" I'd counter.

"It's not the performance, François. It's about people. You can't put a number on it."

Nevertheless, I was learning. I had a chance to test my people skills when Christian had to leave on a last-minute trip to Paris and tasked me with handling a meeting with a woman whom we'll call Esther. Esther was a quintessential "eccentric (moderately) rich lady," prone to charming but odd non sequiturs and more inclined to spend meetings talking about her visions (not her goals, mind you, but her actual dreams) rather than portfolio allocation.

"I'm worried about my finances," she said, finally getting to the point once her oneiric flight of fancy had concluded. "I need my money to grow, but you should only buy companies that will go up. I can't afford to lose any money."

If I knew the secret to picking winners always and without fail, I could wrap this book up after three chapters. But that is not something any advisor can ever guarantee.

I should have been more direct with her, but I still hadn't developed the confidence to tell her plainly, "What you're asking for is impossible." Knowing that I was still young and inexperienced in their eyes, I was eager to prove my worth to her, to Christian, to the firm, to myself. I didn't *promise* her something I might or might not be able to fulfill, but I let her depart the office with an overconfidence in my capacity to deliver.

As I chewed through stacks of annual reports in search of a solid value buy for Esther's portfolio, I came across a small manufacturer of fuel valves called Tokheim. It was little-known but seemed promising: the balance sheet was clean, and the price was low, as was often the case for neglected companies—either too small or not glamorous enough to warrant the attention of security analysts.

It was autumn then, crisp and golden. October is a beautiful month in New York, and the evening was uncharacteristically warm, like a thick velveteen blanket had been wrapped around the island.

At the restaurant, I could tell he was holding something back; there was something he wanted to say. I waited for him to speak.

"I've been missing a lot of work lately, as you know. The doctors examined me last week. There's a small bone pressing against a spinal nerve that's been causing the pain."

"That's awful, Christian. What can they do?"

"They can fix it," he said. "But it's not just that. I have cancer of the kidney."

I was devastated by the news which he delivered so stoically (he was always so calm and even-tempered). He underwent surgery to remove the cancer shortly thereafter, and though it was successful, the nerve in the back had been damaged irreparably. He spent the next several years in constant pain, which curtailed his travels and forced him to come to work less and less. Never had his corner office, which he occupied with an aura of gravitas and esteem, looked so empty.

Meanwhile, I continued my ascent in Tucker Anthony, and by 1980 I had become the vice chairman of the Tucker Anthony Management Corporation. I had also made a name for myself by writing a series of commentaries for clients about the current economic and financial situation and what we were doing about it as investors. Tucker Anthony soon decided to publish them for the firm's clients at large and asked me to work with the firm's reputed strategist, Stanley Berge.

Then, in 1981, the news we had all been dreading finally came. I received word that Christian succumbed to his illness while settling some estate matters in Bermuda. Needless to say, it was a crushing blow to the morale of the firm, and I was at a great loss.

Christian had been with me since the beginning—since *before* the beginning, that moment when I met him upon returning from that snowed-in ski lodge over a decade ago. Peering into his office and knowing that he'd never return, that there would be no more after-hours discussions, that we'd never exchange another word—it was difficult.

But he had taught me well. And I was the natural heir to his extensive list of clients. I was confident I could serve them as well as he had. The question was: were they equally confident in *me*?

Christian had talked to me about his clients often, but I had personally met very few of them, so when it came time for me to reach out to them, most of them regarded me as a stranger, even if I had Christian's tacit posthumous blessing.

When someone dies, his friends and associates will hopefully rally to take care of his unfinished business. It is perhaps the measure of a life well lived if those whom you have left behind care enough to preserve your memory, uphold your reputation, and see to your affairs.

Paul Saurel was a distinguished trust lawyer widely admired in New York and beyond for his legal brilliance, and he and Christian were very close. In fact, Paul was like a second father to him. Paul understood that many of Christian's clients were loyal to Christian, not to the firm, and certainly not to me.

In the months after Christian's death, Paul spent countless hours describing to me the trusts he had created with Christian for their clients, how they had been written, and why. Then, at his own expense, Paul traveled to Europe to confer with those clients and persuade them to stay on with me. And in New York, he and I spent hours with local clients doing the same. (My role was mostly passive during those meetings, as he did most of the talking, so I took notes. I thought I was being dutiful, but he quickly told me to put my pen down and just listen. "Don't take notes in here," he said. "You can ask me questions later if you don't understand something.")

Between the trip to Europe and the meetings in New York, Paul spent untold hours helping me preserve Christian's book of business.

I know he didn't do it for me—he told me as much when I told him I could never thank him enough: "I didn't do it for you. I did it for Christian's memory."

Yet despite his curt way of speaking, in the end, Paul and I also bonded, and Régine and I befriended him and his wife. One remarkable thing about Paul was that he had become partially deaf early in his career. It kept him out of the courtroom, but it didn't inhibit his sparkling legal career or verbal aptitude: just forced him to transition to estate law. As a result of his hearing loss, he was prone to pronouncing words a little awkwardly. So the first time my wife and I had dinner at the Saurels' home was a bit vexing for Régine, who had trouble understanding him, and she was desperate to be nice to him because she knew exactly how good he had been to me.

Paul sat next to Régine at dinner, but I could see the look of panic on her face as she strained to converse. I don't think she understood half the things he said.

"All this time in America, and I thought I knew English well!" she told me later that night. I laughed and told her that it wasn't her fault.

A Multigenerational Legacy

Some of the clients I inherited from Christian still make up a big part of my business today, including several of their children and even grandchildren. Sicart Associates (the company I run today along with a few partners) is not just a money management firm; it's an enterprise that helps people build multigenerational wealth, which I'll discuss further in later chapters.

One such person is Christian's brother, who was also a partner at Tucker Anthony. One might have expected him to become jealous of the attention Christian showed me, or the fact that I inherited Christian's book of business, but he never showed anything but happiness for my success, and we remained good friends until his own death several years ago.

* * *

People stay with you because they feel that you care about them. They trust you. In order to serve clients, you must understand their whole situation. In order to do this, the clients must be willing to talk to you. Otherwise, all that you can talk about is performance. They also are not interested in what you do for other clients: they like to remain under the impression that they are constantly on your mind and the only ones there.

One of my earliest and most successful clients once told me after I bragged about being interviewed on TV: "I am glad for you, but it does not make me feel especially good. As a client, I expect to have privileged access to your ideas and not share them with the public at large."

Most of the time, if a client leaves, it's not because of your performance—unless it is really atrocious. They leave because they don't think you care for them. And if performance is the only thing keeping them there, they're probably not great clients, because there's always going to be someone out there who performs better than you over given periods of time. If performance over part of a cycle is all they value, they'll drop you quickly as a manager when someone temporarily does better.

CHAPTER 4

Contrarian Investing in America

CHRISTIAN HAD HAD SUCH a strong influence over my own career that his death dramatically shook things up for me. If he were still alive, I likely would have remained his right-hand man for years, as I was happy in the role. But in his absence, I had to review my career plan.

As I was a junior partner, I had little influence over the process of merging the two firms, but the acquisition went smoothly, and the new people we were working under were friendly and professional. There was little of the jostling and awkward adjustment that sometimes accompanies mergers.

However, I felt ready to start my own investment firm. I hadn't come all the way to America just to work for a large insurance company. And I told the top people at John Hancock as much. In hindsight, that was an audacious, perhaps even arrogant thing to say, but they didn't take it personally and respected my entrepreneurial ambitions.

Still, although the executives didn't want to stand in my way, they understandably expressed reservations about a partner of the firm they had just acquired immediately jumping ship to start his own company. After some back and forth, we arrived at a compromise: they would allow me to found my own business, but as a subsidiary of John Hancock. They would own 100 percent of it, but I would take home 100 percent of the profits and losses until things had settled down, at which point they would help me become independent. It was a creative arrangement for an unusual, transitional time, but it worked well for both parties. For several years I operated in this fashion until my company became fully independent, John Hancock actually putting a small but symbolically significant token into our capital.

I settled on the name Tocqueville Asset Management. Alexis de Tocqueville was perhaps less well known in his native land than in America where I learned, after I arrived in '69, that his famous work *Democracy in America* was a watershed publication (and still widely studied by high school and university students today).

I actually hadn't read Tocqueville myself until my associate Jean-Pierre Conreur brought me a little book called *The Best of Tocqueville*, or something like that. It was just a primer, not even one hundred pages long, but I was astounded by the prescience and perspicacity of its author. Tocqueville was not only a keen observer and brilliant political analyst but ahead of his time, too, writing about things that were not fashionable in the early nineteenth century, such as the role of women in politics and society and the alienation of manual workers.

So, in naming the company, I piggybacked on Tocqueville's historic reputation, though not without some initial hesitation from his heirs in France, who insisted on meeting with us to ensure we were "good people."

The "us," by the way, was at first a very small team. I hired a couple of smart analysts, graduates of a Columbia University master's program that merged political science and business, and a pair of assistants, and that was it. Initially I was the sole shareholder, but eventually I gave stock to the employees, as I was already convinced that a professional service firm should belong to the people who are on the frontline with its clients.

Since Christian's clients remained with me, initially probably out of inertia rather than conviction, my income essentially tripled overnight. This was an auspicious beginning, as it meant I didn't have to start from scratch building a clientele. And there was something poignant about Christian posthumously giving me a leg up in a new venture just as he had enabled my entrée into Wall Street on my first visit to America.

However, although things got up and running with relative ease, I suddenly felt lonely at the helm. It was a loneliness I hadn't experienced in my career. Not only was I having to manage people for the first time, but I no longer had the benefit of Christian's mentorship or his stalwart presence a few doors down. For the first time, I was really going it alone.

I was free to call the shots and direct the company as I wished, but that brought challenges of its own. To quote Tocqueville himself, "Nothing is more wonderful than the art of being free, but nothing is harder to learn how to use than freedom."

Small Firm, Big Ideas

In any event, there wasn't much time to ruminate on my feelings of solitude. There was work to be done.

Besides undertaking the usual business of growing our clients' money, our most exciting initiative was a research project that helped put our young company on the map.

This series of publications, which was initially marketed to clients and associates before its circulation expanded to other parties, examined different facets of economics and finance. We did so with academic rigor on par with any scholarly journal, but since it was our own project, we had full editorial control and enjoyed the freedom to write or invite experts to write about whatever we wanted.

For example, one popular series of articles was called "Parallels," where invited historians discussed commonalities between previous economic eras and the current one, drawing on the lessons of the past to inform investment decisions today. One memorable project involved working with Dr. Charles Kindleberger, the US expert on many things historical and especially the Great Depression, on a paper analyzing whether another depression was on the horizon.

During our discussions, I raised the question of the "shape" of history. Mark Twain is reputed to have said, "History doesn't repeat itself, but it often rhymes." I had an idea on the reason: history progresses in a spiral.

In the graphic on the next page, for example, point B will display enough similarities with point A that economists with a good memory will experience a strong sense of déjà vu.

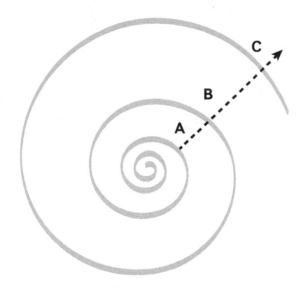

Yet between these two periods, many structural changes will have taken place throughout society, in world trade and in technology, for example. As a result, point B will resemble point A, but it will also be different in enough respects that precisely forecasting what B will look like or exactly when it will occur is very difficult. The only certainty is that there will be a point B and that it will probably "rhyme" with A.

Professor Kindleberger initially seemed to disagree with me on the shape of history. Unfortunately, just as we were putting the last touches to his article, his wife fell ill, and we never completed that discussion.

As our research garnered more interest around Wall Street, we took on one of the big stories of the '80s, which was the purported death of American manufacturing. If you lived through that era, you probably recall grim headlines and frequent imagery of stagnant factories gathering rust while Japan was conquering the world's markets.

Times were indeed tough: the United States endured a difficult recession that ended in 1982, when unemployment hit double digits.

A rise in interest rates appreciated the US dollar, which made it difficult for manufacturers to compete internationally.

However, while American industry had indisputably declined from its peak, the news of its demise, to again paraphrase Mark Twain, had been greatly exaggerated. We took the contrarian position that there actually were signs of an industrial renaissance amid the tumult—if not yet visible in statistics, clearly discernable if you bothered to visit plant floors around the country.

One of our groundbreaking studies argued that the manufacturing sector was not simply dying off but rather *being reborn*. This research drew attention from leading professors as well as the business press, and that year I was invited to speak at the National Association of Manufacturers, the only finance guy in attendance. I also made a few TV appearances to comment on American industry and other issues of the day.

One of my more memorable speaking engagements took place at the Japanese Chamber of Commerce and Industry in New York. The counterpoint to America's economic struggles in the early '80s was Japan, whose thriving economy, some experts feared, threatened the United States' economic predominance. That narrative wasn't without merit: Japan was booming during that period. Its growth was white-hot, and its unemployment was half of that of the United States. Japanese productivity soared in the '80s, which lowered the cost of its exports, and many American firms in multiple industries struggled to compete.

However, all these pronouncements about the Japanese economic powerhouse and moribund American manufacturing were short-sighted, and we at Tocqueville were among the few who made this assertion.

This was the context in which I stepped up to the podium to give my address to the Japanese Chamber. "You will eventually become more like us while we will be catching up with your manufacturing leadership or even surpassing it," I warned.

There were no questions from the audience, and I was not invited back, so I assume the talk was not a hit.

Delivering hard truths is a poor way to please the crowd, but I wasn't there to entertain. I did not make any friends that day, but I ultimately was vindicated, since American manufacturing did bounce back in the '90s, a boom time for the US economy, while Japan endured its painful "lost decade."

> **The pendulum swings one way, and then it swings back again. So much of my success as an investor has been owed to understanding this simple law of economic thermodynamics and taking advantage of the opportunities that the back-and-forth brings.**

This is the great, sweeping ebb and flow of the capital markets, a tale as old as capitalism itself. The pendulum swings one way, and then it swings back again. So much of my success as an investor has been owed to understanding this simple law of economic thermodynamics and taking advantage of the opportunities that the back-and-forth brings.

In those first few years, we weren't making much money, as most of whatever profit we earned went straight back into our research project. But we were on our way, and I was confident in our prospects of long-term success. The research project helped establish us as an intellectual leader in the industry: a young company unafraid to take bold stances and defend them with facts and reason.

We continued to work alongside some of the big names in academia and investing. Robert Kaplan, the well-known professor of accounting at Harvard Business School, became one of our consultants after being impressed with our work.

Professor Kaplan explained to our analysts that traditional management accounting had been developed when materials and direct (manual) labor made up the bulk of manufacturing companies' costs. Those were relatively easy to measure, and the practice developed of allocating so-called overhead or indirect costs, such as marketing, R&D, and administration, in the same proportions as those easily-allocated direct costs. But as industrial activities became lighter, cost structures evolved: by the 1980s, for example, in the growing electronics industry, materials and direct labor no longer represented more than 10 percent to 15 percent of total costs.

As Professor Kaplan explained, US companies were still using a nineteenth-century accounting framework to measure their activities in the twentieth and soon-to-come twenty-first centuries. This misallocation led to misguided investment decisions and, in the aggregate, the wrong assessment of US competitiveness.

Phil Fisher, the guru of growth investing, had also seen one of our articles, and he called me up one day to invite me to visit a company he was analyzing in California. I remember how Phil was avowedly low-tech. He had no computer or quote machine and would glean most of his information from reading annual reports and talking to managements. We had a fantastic day-long visit, during which we got to meet all the executives of that company and query them on all aspects of their business. Those early associations and collaborations with some of these financial luminaries certainly contributed to our firm's early success.

The investment philosophy behind Tocqueville had not changed much from what I had been doing consistently since the late '60s—finding good companies for cheap. In time, we became more contrarian as the industry evolved; information spread faster and more broadly so that you had to work harder and harder to locate assets that offered good value. But by and large, the same disciplines that had been taught to me by my early mentors formed the core of our business.

Work and Play

I wasn't the only Sicart who was thriving as an entrepreneur. By now Régine's dressmaking business had blossomed, and just as Tocqueville Asset Management was making a name for itself on Wall Street, she had carved out a prestigious niche in the competitive New York fashion industry, actually appearing on the front page of *Women's Wear Daily* in a photo of America's most promising new designers.

Socially, her circle mostly consisted of her Park Avenue lady customers and their husbands. We were also friends with the owner of a well-known art gallery who often invited us to openings, and through our connections with the worlds of finance and fashion, we did have the chance to meet some interesting people.

Usually at these gatherings, I didn't really know anybody, and even when I did, I often forgot I had met them before!

I do recall one amusing encounter. At dinner one evening, I was seated next to a charming young woman.

"And what do you do for a living?" I asked.

"Oh, I'm an actress," she said nonchalantly.

CHAPTER 5

Market Bubbles
and Crashes

THE MARKET WILL TEST your mettle. In boom times, it's a seductive siren tempting you to cough up more capital, even when your gut (not to mention the data) tells you prices are high. In the depth of a bear market, you'll be whiplashed with fear that your existing portfolio will never recover and that any new investments are fraught with risk.

In truth, it's when prices are low that the risk is minimized, and when they're soaring that risk is magnified, but emotions (yours as well as your clients' and colleagues') will get in your head and short-circuit your rational thought process so that up starts looking down, and down looks up.

Just like Eros and Thanatos—the love instinct and the death instinct—are, according to Freud, the two life forces that govern human behavior, greed and fear are the two poles of market psychology. The market is like a grand pendulum swinging between panic and euphoria, taking us all along for the ride. As this chapter will examine, an investor must understand both fundamentals and psychology to succeed. Anyone can achieve limited success over a period of months or years, but to deliver sustainable results over a long time line, one must subordinate their emotions to rational thought and long-term principles.

It's easier said than done: the base emotions of fear and greed exert a powerful grip on even seasoned investors. Not only must one temper their emotions in the face of extreme upward and downward moves, but they must train themselves to remain fixed on the long term and be unaffected by the daily, weekly, or monthly vicissitudes of the market.

Keeping a cool head in the face of spastic, drastic ups and downs while suppressing the human tendency toward shortsightedness and near-term thinking is one of the great challenges for a wealth manager, which is why people entrust us to safeguard their family's assets.

For us contrarian investors, the challenge is even greater. We make money by doing one thing when everyone else is doing another—the lone boat beating against the tide. Few can do it well. But those who can are rewarded handsomely, building great wealth and achieving— over the cycles—the kind of market-beating returns that elude so many Wall Street professionals with shorter-term horizons.

After a half century of having a front-row seat to the cyclical drama of the financial markets, I've witnessed it all: bulls that beget bears that beget bulls that beget bears; insane bubbles; agonizing crashes; fortunes made and lost and recaptured; global panic; intoxicating euphoria; and everything in between.

The Swinging Sixties

Capitalism, like many other systems both natural and man-made, undergoes a continual process of growth and contraction, creation and destruction—the economic cycle with which we are all familiar. As nations industrialized in the eighteenth and nineteenth centuries, these cycles seemed to grow more extreme, and each ensuing depression became more destructive. But by the twentieth century, states began to manage fiscal and monetary policy in a way that seemed to permit more control over the economy and some regulation of this cyclical process.

By the postwar era, in the United States, some experts were claiming that we had mastered fiscal and monetary policy so adroitly that we had conquered the economic cycle for good; recessions, they said, were a thing of the past. This pronouncement was a little myopic, as the country did experience several recessions after 1950 (in 1953, 1957, and 1960), but these were relatively brief and mild (unemployment never exceeded 7.5 percent), and the United States was such an economic dynamo in the 1950s that rosy pronouncements about "the end of recessions" might have been forgiven.

This typically American brand of boundless (perhaps a little irrational) optimism continued into the 1960s, and from 1961 to 1969, the economy blossomed and the stock market rose irrepressibly. It seemed like it might never end, like we truly were living in an unprecedented era of limitless prosperity. In hindsight, such beliefs seem naïve, and even though I was a novice in the late '60s, they seemed naïve to me too. Any good investor knows that it's precisely in these moments of bliss when you must be most cautious.

Such was the climate in which I started my tenure at Tucker Anthony. I was fortunate that some of my early mentors were contrarians who were—as Warren Buffett's oft-quoted axiom goes—greedy when others were fearful, and fearful when others were greedy. And many people were greedy in 1969, as they are in any stubborn bull market.

once jokingly advised: "Take all your savings and buy some good stock and hold it till it goes up, then sell it. If it don't go up, don't buy it." Investors remain oblivious to, or choose to ignore, the risk on the presumption that the price will continue its climb. They reason that they'll get out at the first sign of danger or as soon as the top blows off. No one ever thinks he'll be the "greatest fool," but of course someone always ends up holding the bag.

It's a Faustian bargain—make a deal with the devil, and the devil comes for his due. When the market crashed in 1973, the fallout was swift and nasty, initiating one of the worst bear markets of the twentieth century. Some companies that had weathered the recession are still household names (Texas Instruments, Black & Decker), while others have since faded into obsolescence (Emery Air Freight). The Dow Jones Industrial Average (DJIA) lost nearly half its value, and the Nifty Fifty tumbled like a house of cards. Xerox lost 71 percent, Avon 86 percent, and Polaroid 91 percent. The Vestal Virgins had been defiled, not by lust but by greed—the deadliest of investment sins. Some of these companies' stock prices didn't recover until the next decade.

Ironically, the popularity of the Nifty Fifty as "recession resistant" ended up contributing to the very economic misery that investors hoped to avoid, because as investors flooded them with cash, they helped create an asset bubble—and bubbles always burst eventually.

What was notable about the ensuing recession was how wide-spread it was—in the United States, seemingly no company or sector managed to escape its wrath, and abroad, every industrialized nation was afflicted. Economic misery loves company. This was a global recession, nastier than the previous domestic one and, because it spilled over borders, that made it harder for nation-states to rein it in using the policy tools at their disposal.

For us, however, there were some silver linings. In the late '60s, Christian had invested heavily in natural resources, including gold, copper, uranium, oil, and sugar. For a few years, the prices mostly remained static, but around 1973, aided by the decision to let the dollar float down, there was a big spike in inflation, and commodities, especially silver and gold, did very well. So in the first year of the bear market, our portfolios actually held their ground, even as the rest of the market was collapsing.

Oil, in particular, ended up performing especially well, because October 1973 brought the first of two major disruptions to the worldwide petroleum market. It happened when, in response to political and diplomatic events in the Middle East, the Organization of the Petroleum Exporting Countries (OPEC) instituted an embargo that quadrupled the price of oil virtually overnight and sent shockwaves throughout an already reeling global economy. Most investors suffered, but those of us who had been in oil profited nicely.

After the so-called oil shock, it was evident the game had changed; the politics of oil would perennially have immense impact on economic affairs, and OPEC itself was a politico-economic force to be reckoned with. But incredibly, some experts still downplayed the near-term impact of the event. I remember that during the crisis, I was attending a meeting of the New York Society of Security Analysts, and there were three famous economists who all said, "The tripling of oil and the OPEC creation doesn't change anything in our forecasts."

That was when I decided to visit the Middle East for the first time. In very early 1974, I met economists, politicians, and business-people in Lebanon, Kuwait, and Iran. I had lunch in Kuwait with a leading Saudi businessman and asked, "I had no time to arrange a trip to Saudi Arabia, and I would like to return soon with my wife. However, she is Jewish: do you think that would be a problem?"

His answer was, "To start with, they will ask why you want to bring your wife."

The experienced showed me that, as happened to me in China a few years later, early travelers to a little-visited land can get answers to questions that they might not dare ask later. The 1974 trip clearly showed that the world financial system and economy would be changed for years to come. But it also made it clear that the quadrupling of the oil price had not yet had an impact so that the US economists were right in the immediate term and totally wrong for the future.

What resulted, in fact, was a curious coincidence of both inflation and deflation. The sudden rise in oil prices increased the cost of production across the board but at the same time acted as a tax on consumers that depressed consumption and economic activity.

By 1975, the recession was over. While much of our portfolio performed poorly, the prescient accumulation of natural resources and our cautious, scaled-down allocation of the high-flying—and hard-crashing—Nifty Fifty enabled us to come out relatively unscathed.

Even though the recession ended in 1975, this was merely the calm before the storm, because four years later, the Iranian revolution produced another sudden contraction of the global oil supply. In fact, as a percentage of total global output, the reduction was negligible, but human psychology is a volatile accelerant that turns a small flame into a conflagration. Global oil markets were plunged into turmoil again, and the price of crude shot up dramatically.

The US economy had already been flashing warning signs (for example, inflation had increased unabated and was at double-digit levels by 1979), but the second oil crisis of the decade tipped things over the edge.

During the 1970s, on subsequent trips to Lebanon and other places in the Middle East to do some on-the-ground research, I was particularly interested in what was going on with the massive accumulation of capital by OPEC countries, which were accumulating so many US dollars (the trading currency of the global energy market) that there was no way they could invest it back into their own countries, as few of them had developed any major industries beyond petroleum. Since oil producers were not keen to be slaves to the US financial markets, a market developed among Europe-based banks to receive the dollars and loan them: the Eurodollar market.

Initially, this was not regulated, without any central bank supervision or reserve requirements. But upon analysis, it became clear that after a first phase when the withdrawn liquidity would be recessionary for the world economy, an inflationary period would follow, as the Eurodollar market would add to the liquidity created by central banks to fight the recessionary tendencies.

In the midst of the Iranian oil crisis, I went on another fact-finding mission to Lebanon to better understand the people as well as the economy of the region. On my return to New York, I authored an extensive study on oil that argued that basically, between the energy-saving efforts on the one hand and the situation in the Middle East, I concluded the game was over for oil.

Christian, whose health was already deteriorating, fiercely contested my conclusion; so much, in fact, that I refrained from publishing that report, which died before it saw the light of day.

After Christian's passing, however, one of the first things I did was sell our energy holdings. The timing was fortunate because oil prices were still high, but the rest of the market was on its way to losing a quarter of its value during the 1981–82 recession. This move left me

I was in London at the time, making presentations to a group of institutional investors, and I heard the news on the hotel lobby television. The computer technology executing buy-and-sell orders was less developed than it is now, so not only had faulty technology contributed to the crash, but a massive influx of orders left the systems overwhelmed and delayed to the point where we actually had no idea what the prices were. It took hours, if not days, to catch up with the trades of that day, leaving investors worldwide in the dark about the value of their portfolio.

Meanwhile, I had to tend to the human side of the business, so I called our clients at the end of the day to reassure them we were in control. Then I called Jean-Pierre Conreur, who was my partner at the time, and asked, "What are you doing?"

"There's nothing we can do because the tape is hours late, and we have no idea what's going on. I'm making lists of things to buy," he said.

The market was just collapsing, but he was keeping his cool, with his eye on the next move. Value investors wait patiently for moments like this. I wasn't thrilled by the precipitous decline across multiple indices, but opportunities emerge amid crises (as long as you have cash on the sidelines to take advantage of them). And you can steel yourself against any anxiety induced by market movement by sticking to your plan. A plan, adhered to consistently and based on a solid investment philosophy, will carry you through turbulent times.

Jean-Pierre had, perhaps, less reason to fret than I did, as I had recently made some moves that now seemed ill-timed. In January 1987, I founded the Tocqueville Fund, a contrarian, value-oriented mutual fund. We didn't do any marketing, so the investors mostly consisted of longtime clients and associates of Tucker Anthony who had known me for almost twenty years and generally trusted my judgement.

The S&P got off to a jackrabbit start in 1987. After five years of consistent gains, I was wary about valuations, signs of a coming economic slowdown, and fallacious promises of "portfolio insurance" through derivatives. Much of the early inflow into the Tocqueville Fund thus stayed largely in cash.

Today's label to justify jumping onto a mad wagon (FOMO, or fear of missing out) had not become popular yet, but as 1987 wound on and the markets continued to climb, I fielded many calls from colleagues and investors who were growing frustrated with their cash sitting idle. Their complaints became a familiar refrain: "If I had wanted to own a money market fund, I would have bought into one!"

Bowing to the pressure, I yielded and invested a sizable portion of the Fund's cash only weeks before Black Monday.

Now that global indices were plummeting, there wasn't much I could do except patiently ride it out.

In the days that followed, as the smoke cleared, we took stock of our situation. When panic strikes, investors sell what they can, and that means larger companies with liquid stocks. Since we held a number of smaller companies which were less liquid, they were initially less vulnerable to the wave of panic selling that continued throughout the week, so at first, we came out relatively unscathed. I thought we were geniuses! But eventually the downward momentum of the market pulled us down along with everyone else, and by November we were faring poorly—a little better than most, but not by much. Still, it could have been worse if we had yielded to the buying pressure from our clients and the markets as a whole in the run-up to October. Another lesson: if you have convictions, holding cash is better than making mistakes.

Black Monday was a black swan, which, by nature, is unpredictable. However, while you can't foresee such events, you can adequately prepare for them and take necessary precautionary measures to defend your portfolio when they come.

The best approach is to heed the warning of Hyman Minsky, who observed that economic and financial stability leads to instability *without the need for an external trigger*, simply by making people more complacent and more willing to accept risk. According to Dr. Minsky, a period of sustained economic and financial stability encourages risk-taking—especially through the growing use of debt—until excess leverage causes a sudden collapse in asset prices, which is a normal part of the credit cycle. Long periods of stability thus naturally lead to instability, though with unpredictable timing.

During a prolonged period of stability, historically, an early indication that a bull market is aging has been when a group of stocks eventually dominates trading volumes, index performances, and the news while the broader market begins to lag. This is referred to as the market lacking breadth. Though this wasn't exactly the case in the late '80s, I've seen it play out several times: in the Nifty Fifty stocks in the 1970s, the internet bubble stocks in the late 1990s, and, as I write this in 2020, the seemingly indomitable FAANG companies: Facebook, Amazon, Apple, Netflix, Google.

On New Year's Eve 1989, Régine and I ended a most eventful decade along with our closest friends, in an impromptu gathering at our Manhattan apartment. As the glittering Times Square ball made its descent, I reflected on all that had happened in the last ten years. I had begun the decade as a junior partner of a firm that now no longer existed, and I had overseen Tocqueville Asset Management from its inception into a highly regarded wealth management firm with its own publicly traded mutual fund.

The '90s would prove to be less tumultuous, but just as challenging. A new era brought new changes. The global economy was evolving rapidly, and Wall Street was right behind, racing to stay ahead of the curve.

The Dot-com Era

In *Extraordinary Popular Delusions and the Madness of Crowds*, published in 1841, Charles Mackay astutely analyzed various speculative bubbles, many with fanciful names like the Mississippi Scheme or the South Sea Bubble. His work remains the basic reference on the enduring propensity of crowds to behave irrationally in financial matters, oscillating between euphoria and panic in recurring cycles.

Mackay's diagnosis of market psychology remains as relevant as ever, and investors in the '90s would have been wise to read more of Mackay and less

Markets change, technologies change, business changes, economies change—but people stay the same. And ultimately, people drive markets.

of, say, *Dow 36,000,* that overly optimistic tome published shortly before the dot-com bubbles burst and whose audacious thesis seems absurd now.

The torrid growth of the markets led by the technology companies of the NASDAQ, which soared 400 percent from 1995 to 2000 before the bubble popped, would not have surprised Mackay. Even though he was writing 150 years earlier, he had seen this pattern play out before. Markets change, technologies change, business changes, economies change—but people stay the same. And ultimately, people drive markets.

prospects affect its stock price, often disproportionately. This makes the risk/reward ratios unacceptable.

The story of radio is instructive: it did change the world and disrupted traditional news and advertising media, and RCA's earnings and stock price exploded accordingly. Yet few of radio's early developers and participants made lasting gains from this, as competition and industry changes eroded the hoped-for profits.

Investors in RCA at the top of the 1929 speculative boom were right about radio's fundamentals: the number of households with radio sets grew from 2.75 million in 1925 to 10.25 million in 1929 and, *through the Great Depression*, to 27.5 million in 1939. But the investors were wrong about RCA's stock price. As we see in the following chart, the fate of AOL's stock following the 1990s dot-com boom was not very different.

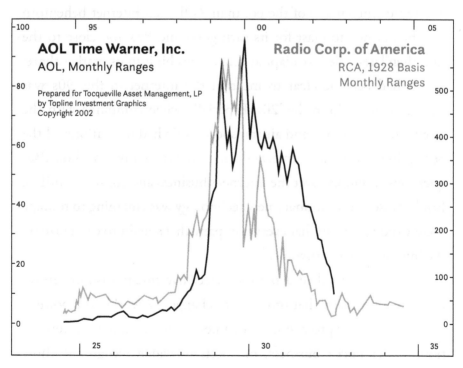

AOL Time Warner, Inc.
AOL, Monthly Ranges

Prepared for Tocqueville Asset Management, LP
by Topline Investment Graphics
Copyright 2002

Radio Corp. of America
RCA, 1928 Basis
Monthly Ranges

You could map a similar chart over any number of other companies that experienced a meteoric rise and an even faster and more dramatic fall in their stock prices. Some of those companies survived; some eventually emerged to become the tech titans that dominate the sector today. But many others never recaptured their highs or even went bankrupt.

All bubbles have a valuable idea or concept at their core. In the 1920s, the 1970s, and the 1990s, these trends were initiated by smart and sophisticated people, experts at articulating the case for the companies or the industries they were promoting. Unfortunately, very smart people are seldom the ones with the most discriminating common sense. The problem arises when a large crowd of investors joins them, understanding the concept but not capable of envisioning second-level effects—including operating or strategic mistakes and disruptive new competition. Those who do this are likely to overpay for their dreams.

Plus ça Change—Same Story, Different Day: A Lifetime of Lessons about the Market

In hindsight, the mania that surrounds bubbles seems so foolish. How did market participants not see the trap they were being lured into? Why do even experienced investors get taken by emotion, somehow believing that this time will be different?

This question can be answered psychologically, but it raises other, more technical/financial questions about the relationship to valuation and price. How do valuations become decoupled from their fundamentals? What, actually, is driving the price of a given stock?

The father of value investing, Benjamin Graham, explained this apparent disconnect by saying that *"in the short run, the market is like a voting machine"* while *"in the long run, the market is like a weighing machine."* The latter is dictated by the company's actual metrics, the former by psychology more than anything else.

Thus, over short or intermediate periods, investors' opinions exert a greater influence on the performance of a stock than the operating or balance sheet statistics of the underlying companies. P/E ratios, for example, fluctuate much more widely than would be justified by company fundamentals alone. Over the very long term (often decades), stock prices tend to track companies' fundamentals (i.e., earnings), which tend to move with sales and assets which, in turn, tend to follow economies' growth rates and productivity.

But company fundamentals change relatively slowly. It makes little sense to attribute stock price changes, even over months, to fundamental progress: what they really are are changes in the price to earnings, where P moves a lot and E relatively little. Such short-term fluctuations are principally due to investors' *perceptions* of probable future developments. These perceptions, as purely psychological phenomena, can be volatile to the point of irrationality.

The real price of a stock is not, of course, its quote in the newspaper, which alone is meaningless, but some valuation measure usually expressed as a ratio of that quote to some fundamental income or balance sheet measure: in an auction market, this reflects the supply and demand for that stock among the mass of investors.

In theory, contrarian investing necessitates buying low (when stocks are not in favor) and selling high (when they are), *as should value investing*. Rising stock prices signify greater risk. Contrarian value investors should become euphoric when the crowd succumbs to panic and cautious when the crowd is taken by reckless exuberance.

However, both approaches (value and contrarian) have lost some of their precision in recent years.

For example, there are natural limits to how high or how low the P/E ratio can go. The P/E ratio should therefore remain within a channel, even if a broad one. Thus investors may not be able to buy at the lowest price or to sell at the exact top but, by following the value discipline, they can improve their odds of success. Unfortunately, to calculate any value ratio, investors need to know the true value of a company's earnings and assets, and that is difficult in the absence of appropriate accounting tools.

My own observation is that, over the near term, stock market fluctuations are perhaps 90 to 100 percent determined by crowd psychology and only 10 to 0 percent by changes in fundamentals. As the time horizon lengthens and the market becomes more of a "weighing machine," the factors influencing stock prices trend toward 90 percent fundamentals and 10 percent psychology.

This means that prudent investors who are keyed in to the incessant back-and-forth movement between panic at the bottom and euphoria at the top can profit handsomely, and as a contrarian investor, I've been doing it for decades. But this approach really is, at its best, only at the climactic extremes of euphoria and depression.

The rest of the time, and particularly over shorter periods, it's at a disadvantage compared to so-called momentum investing. Momentum, however, works best in the short term and thus encourages heavy portfolio turnover. Moreover, it is hard to distinguish between short-term cycles *within* a trend and major reversals in long-term trends.

The contrarian approach tends to function best at extremes of market euphoria and depression. In the absence of guideposts for value (which valuation is supposed to provide), crowd psychology

will have to wait to be right and possibly underperform the market (which does not mean *losing* money most of the time—just making a bit less). This is when bubbles form and grow. But he will catch up and more when those bubbles burst.

> It's a very *human* trait to be swayed by what others are doing and to be seized by emotion in times of euphoria and panic. A long-term investor must develop a bulletproof self-discipline to overcome that tendency.

I am a contrarian because I recognize the madness of crowds. It's easy to be influenced by that madness, as several hundred years of financial history attest. Mimicry—imitating the behavior of others—is encoded in our DNA. It's a product of our evolution (social as well as biological). Simply put, it's a very *human* trait to be swayed by what others are doing and to be seized by emotion in times of euphoria and panic. A long-term investor must develop a bulletproof self-discipline to overcome that tendency.

To complement that self-discipline, one also needs a shrewd analytical mind to pick apart companies and markets. Being a contrarian doesn't mean arbitrarily going against the tide—just because everyone is saying, "It's raining," doesn't mean you go out without an umbrella. You must have the intellectual chops to verify your contrarian thesis by studying the facts and fundamentals—of course, getting this right is one of the hardest parts.

Finally, one's analytical intelligence must be combined with a strong *conviction*. For novices, making decisions based on gut reaction is a quick way to lose your shirt, but the kind of conviction that is cultivated over decades in the business, aided by talented mentors and honed by much trial and error, is priceless. All veterans have it. Those who can't trust their conviction as a complement to their reason and their emotional calm tend not to last.

I have a strong instinct for when things feel right and even more for when they don't. I don't predict trends so much as feel them— often out of a contrarian bias.

As I write this, in the midst of a coronavirus pandemic with no end in sight, the major markets have seesawed from a one-third drop value in March 2020—the fastest decline of such magnitude in US history—to a stunning recovery that has lifted the S&P 500 and especially the NASDAQ to all-time highs. But red flags abound, and many of the same psychological mechanisms I've seen so many times seem to be casting their dangerous spell again as investors blithely ignore the risks.

The more I learn about the investing business, the more I am convinced that the rule of the game is not to try to be right all the time, or even most of the time. Over time, the stock market tends to go up because economies and businesses grow. Our focus, therefore, should not be to guess right but to make money. By and large, this is achieved by losing less money than the majority during the most dangerous times. If you can detect when or where most people are the most foolish and avoid these situations, then just by avoiding these grossest mistakes, you will do better than the majority over time.

CHAPTER 6

Protecting Families, Building a Legacy: Patrimony Management

WILLIAM[1] HAD AMASSED great wealth as an entrepreneur in several businesses, but he had a fractious relationship with his two sons, one of whom he had not spoken with for years for reasons that remained vague even after I had earned the trust of all the parties.

I had observed this pattern before and knew where it was headed. William was getting on in years, and with no resolution to the filial dispute in sight, I worried that this rift would never be healed. William had not stipulated that his sons would receive his money after his passing, and his sons maintained with equal resolve that they didn't want it. Yet I knew both parties would regret it if the matter was left as it was.

After much arguing, I convinced William to donate a fairly large sum to each of his children. As I spoke to them about William's

---

1   A pseudonym, of course.

and economic trends while leaving client relations to him. When I inherited his business and struck out on my own as the head of a new firm, I quickly learned that relationships are not secondary to performance. On the contrary, a client will rarely leave you because of performance alone. But if they feel you don't care about them, they grow dissatisfied, and they start looking for someone who does.

This part of the business requires empathizing with their emotional needs and understanding their lives and personalities intimately. What do they desire (and fear) most in life? What is important to them? What is their personal history, and what kind of future do they envision for themselves? For their children? Their children's children and beyond? All these factors dictate how we serve them as patrimony managers. Our ability to help them is contingent on knowing their situation inside out and empathizing with their deepest-held concerns and values.

Talking About Money

Our dedication to patrimony management is reflected in the fact that most of our clients are families rather than individuals. Many of them have been with us for decades, and their trust in us is evidenced by the fact that we don't have a slice of their fortune—we manage *all* of their assets. And of course we produce strong returns to justify their loyalty, but that trust is rooted in something bigger than figures and percentages.

One way we help families is by facilitating difficult discussions about money, including estate planning. In most families, money is a touchy subject that everyone prefers to avoid. The parents don't want to talk about it because they think their children are children even when they are fifty or sixty years old. And the children fear that if they ask about it, they'll be perceived as covetous of their parents' wealth.

Many fortune holders are afraid to tell their children about the size of the family fortune because they often prefer to raise their children under the pretense that they do not have more money than their friends and will have to prepare for a life of hard work and self-reliance. Still others like to wield money as a tool of power even as their children are well into adulthood, understanding that the threat of access to the family fortune can force compliance with the parents' certain wishes. Whatever the motivation, important questions tend to remain unresolved—often until it's too late.

As wealth managers, we help break the impasse around these vital talks about inheritances and other financial concerns by stepping in as a kind of mediator. It's a powerful moment when you finally get everyone to sit down at the table and engage with the issue head-on.

Most families, when they finally get around to it, handle these talks harmoniously and diplomatically. In some cases, however, it becomes a contest of competing interests as various parties lay claim to what they feel is theirs. Long-festering tensions between relatives (which may have their origin in affairs that are completely unrelated to finances) may manifest. The dialogue can become acrimonious—infrequently, but I've seen it happen.

I myself don't have an agenda, or rather, my agenda is simply to do what's best for the family as a whole. It's essential that if a third party is brokering the discussion about finances or estate planning, it is someone with no vested interest in the outcome. I recall how, very early in my career, I became cotrustee (along with a lawyer appointed by the family) of a trust for three ladies who had lost a lot of money because the previous trustee had mismanaged their assets. But I sensed the lawyer who replaced him was still mixing his own interests with those of the clients, which tainted the process, so I resigned.

Talking about money is uncomfortable generally, but discussing inheritance is especially difficult because of the subtext of mortality. Few people want to openly confront the prospect of their own passing, and children in particular don't want to think seriously about the day when their parents will leave them.

In other cases, discussing inheritance may stir up a confrontation about firmly held beliefs about entitlement, desert (who deserves what), legacy, and tradition. Sometimes inheritors feel like they have a larger claim to the family patrimony than perhaps their parents are willing to give.

Every family situation is different, but the solution to mediate these disputes is the same: talk it out. Come to an agreement, or at least an understanding. But do it sooner rather than later.

One of the biggest and unfortunately most common mistakes is to wait to have this talk until a parent dies. It's not enough to let the will or the trust do all the work. That's merely a legal document to dictate the distribution of assets. A will doesn't satisfy the social/ emotional task of candid discourse so the parents can explain what they are leaving behind and to whom.

Inheritance isn't the only concern either: children also want to be reassured their parents will have enough to live comfortably in retirement. This is not as much of a concern among high net worth families, but the best course of action is not to make assumptions.

At Sicart Associates (the company I founded after Tocqueville, which I'll discuss in the following chapter), we have a dedicated specialist, Patsy Jaganath, who, along with two or three attorneys we work with, assists families in managing the ins and outs of wills, inheritances, and trusts. As our clients are based not only in the United

States but also in Europe, Latin America, and Asia, we're proficient at managing the complex legal, technical, and tax issues of different jurisdictions.

One challenge of estate planning is that it is conducted at that fraught point where questions of money collide with weighty, emotionally charged issues like life, death, family, and ownership or entitlement. And few things stir up strong feelings like assets of great sentimental importance, especially if one has grown up with them (or *in* them, in the case of a family home) or if they've been handed down from one generation to the next. If these assets are also priceless, they can produce a volatile disagreement among heirs.

Real estate, art, jewelry, antiques, and heirlooms of various types often become points of contention as they change hands. Not only do these assets sometimes inspire a great deal of sentimental attachment, they're highly illiquid. You can't tear an oil painting down the middle and give one-half to each child. And how does one bequeath a house, which can be split in two no more easily than the painting? Co-ownership by multiple children is not necessarily a good option, since it only introduces questions of who is responsible for what in maintaining the house, and is especially unfeasible if one child has a warmhearted attachment to the property and can't bear the thought of relinquishing while the other simply sees it as just another asset—or perhaps even a liability—in the portfolio.

And real estate can indeed be a liability, especially if it's not generating income to offset the ongoing expense of upkeep and taxes, which can be monstrously expensive if the house is opulent, historic, or both.

As many of our European clients descend from aristocratic lineages, they have real estate holdings that have been in the family for generations, if not centuries—castles, manors, and other baronial estates. A castle, despite its romantic, historical grandeur, is frequently an impractical bequest. It is burdensome and expensive to maintain. It may be remotely located, far from any of the surviving children, and is likely to sit empty for most of the year. The younger generation may not feel personally attached to it, especially if they weren't raised there. But other members of the family may consider sacrilegious the suggestion that an heirloom property be sold away—to do so, they may argue, would be to sully the family name and the legacy of their forebears.

Such are the arguments that arise when parents pass title to the next generation. This is why it's essential to discuss these things as early as possible. Don't wait for these issues to come spilling out during the reading of the will.

The approach I recommend to the question of property holdings may not be the most sentimental, but it is the simplest one, and the one that causes the least amount of acrimony: liquidate them before you pass (or instruct the executor or trustee to do so after death). Cash is a lot more fungible, and a lot less complicated, than a castle. (In the medieval and Renaissance periods, European families spent centuries fighting among and between each other over control of such estates—that is one tradition that need not be perpetuated within your own family.) Selling these properties will save a lot of headache and potentially bitter discussions among your inheritors. If they're so enthused about real estate, they can always reinvest the money they inherit in another property of their choosing.

The Third-Generation Curse

In every family, there are spenders and savers. Savers protect but do not fixate on their capital. They don't touch it. They don't move it around. They don't trade and speculate with it. They leave it to grow.

Certainly they don't make lavish, frivolous expenditures they can't afford. Over time, the savers always win.

The spenders are ones who see money as a way to assert themselves or to demonstrate or seek power. Consequently, they always buy property at the wrong time, usually because they want to impress other people or to inflate their own self-importance. Spenders usually end up selling at the wrong time too.

They evince similar behavior in other markets: for example, always being sucked in by the hoopla around the latest hot stock being trumpeted in the financial press. In short, they take unnecessary risks and possess an overconfident belief in their entrepreneurial acumen.

Spenders always end up being the losers (financially speaking) in the family—and every family has at least one. Usually, these people are members of the third generation.

What the first generation spends a lifetime building, the third generation squanders. A famous American proverb says, "From shirtsleeves to shirtsleeves in three generations." In Japan, it's "Rice paddies to rice paddies in three generations"; "Clogs to clogs in only three generations" in England; "Wealth never survives three generations" in China; and in Scotland, "The father buys, the son builds, the grandchild sells, and his son begs."

The "third-generation curse" seems to be a universal phenomenon. In studying transgenerational family dynamics, it isn't hard to see why.

First-generation fortune builders usually had an original, often disruptive idea. They may have been immigrants (as is often the case in the United States) and thus had to surmount the barriers and prejudices associated with their origins. Many simply opted to do things differently, either in their neighborhood or in their industry. But as a rule, most founders of multigenerational fortunes overcame significant odds. Their overriding incentive was to survive this adversity and, willingly or not, *they succeeded by being different.*

The following generations, in contrast, were eager *not* to differentiate too much from their friends and neighbors. This conformity surely brought a sense of comfort, belonging, and status, but at a price: the second generation becomes a little *too* comfortable.

However, fortunately, members of the second generation are often close enough to the first generation creators of the family fortune to realize that they might not possess the entrepreneurial talent and the single-minded drive to achieve what their parents did without help. And they grow up listening to stories about the toil and the tears, the stress and strife their mother and father endured to elevate the family into the upper echelon.

Consequently, the second generation holds as sacrosanct the responsibility for preserving the patrimony that is left in their custody, for the use of future generations and in deference to the preceding one.

Practically speaking, maintaining wealth is a greater challenge than one may expect. Years ago, a client member of a second generation instructed me, "All I want is to leave my two sons a fortune equivalent to what I received after taxes and the erosion in purchasing power due to inflation." When I attempted to calculate the extent of the damage imposed by 40 percent inheritance taxes and 5 percent annual inflation, $100 would only be worth $15 in purchasing power for each son after fifteen years. Achieving my client's goal would have required *an annual investment return of nearly 14 percent—almost unheard of over a long period of time, and certainly beyond what any advisor can guarantee.*

The risk is multiplied by the time the third generation comes around. By this point in time, they're far removed from the toil, sacrifice, and ambition of their grandparents. They probably grow up in luxury and thus take for granted that the nice things and carefree lifestyle they enjoy are the product of their progenitors' moderation.

Nor do they share the sense of obligation that characterizes the second generation. Instead that responsibility has been replaced by a feeling of entitlement—the family fortune has been built and preserved *for them*. It is their birthright.

Third generationers who, thanks to the efforts of the first and second generationers, have met few obstacles in their youth might see their efforts in life as greater than those of others while this is not as others see it. Many philosophers, starting with Aristotle, have advised: "Knowing yourself is the beginning of all wisdom." Today, we call this *introspection*, and this study of oneself is a discipline that some third generationers do not know how to practice without prejudice.

As a result, it's easier for them to make wrong life and career decisions: for example, wrongly believing that they understand real estate while buying and selling their houses at the wrong time; taking investment dives in venture capital, attracted by the prospect of huge, rapid fortunes but unaware of the work and skills required, etc. Meanwhile, a pervasive sense of entitlement makes third generationers impatient to get their hands on the family fortune, to start enjoying the free-spending and power that they will inherit with it.

And because they have not experienced and do not fear a lack, do not know what it means to go without, they are not as motivated as their predecessors to work harder than most of their peers for what they want.

An additional factor is that, in recent decades, life expectancies have been steadily increasing in most of the world. Generations now tend to last longer, as does their control of family patrimonies. Not surprisingly, third-generation members often become impatient to assume the privileges, if not the responsibilities, that they perceive previous generations to have effortlessly enjoyed.

Perhaps the fault is not all theirs, for if their parents (the second generation) have failed to discuss money matters with them, how are they supposed to learn otherwise?

Moreover, to be fair, the third generation that is finding their way in the world today—millennials and Generation Z—faces more downward pressure than their parents encountered, a reversal in some respects of the "each generation has it easier than the last" pattern that has defined American life for at least a century. Increasing educational expenses, a higher cost of living (especially for healthcare and housing), and flatlining wages make it so that the third generation not only has a different view of and relationship to their wealth, but they're also spending and saving it in an entirely different environment than their grandparents and even parents were.

> **Effective patrimony management is a matter of loyalty and longevity— the mutual loyalty that grows between advisors and families who trust and respect each other and the longevity cultivated by decades of fruitful collaboration.**

So, left to their own devices, the third generation is vulnerable to eroding that legacy. Wealth is like trust or a reputation: it takes years of patient attention to grow but can be destroyed with alarming rapidity. If the third generation has not been raised to appreciate the value of money, saving and investing, or the virtue of purposeful work, or the great responsibility involved in preserving a fortune, or cannot overcome the structural barriers and socioeconomic challenges of the present moment, the family patrimony is imperiled.

This is why the steward of wealth is best equipped to serve as guardian of the family assets and facilitator of vital discussions and, if need be, mediator of disputes over estate planning and other concerns.

Effective patrimony management is a matter of loyalty and longevity—the mutual loyalty that grows between advisors and families who trust and respect each other and the longevity cultivated by decades of fruitful collaboration. From an investment standpoint, it is running a marathon rather than a sprint. Those who are distracted by short-term market fluctuations—treating the project of wealth-building like a series of sprints—are bound to lag behind the marathon runners. Indeed, very few sprinters can keep up that torrid pace.

Besides a long-term investment strategy, you need someone who can navigate complex family dynamics to bring everyone to the table and facilitate (or force, if need be) the vital discussion that no one wants to have, but which everyone will regret putting off if they postpone it too long.

This kind of assiduous attention to families (not just portfolios) is what distinguishes smaller firms from larger companies and what inspired me to found Sicart Associates, which you'll hear more about in the coming chapter.

CHAPTER 7

The Homme D'Affaires

SICART ASSOCIATES WAS BORN on the spur of the moment, though for quite some time, I had complained to my main partners at Tocqueville Asset Management that we had grown too much too fast. In my view, that growth had resulted in a dilution of our culture, which had been built on a combination of talent, principles, team spirit, spontaneity, and congeniality.

In the thirty-odd years since I'd created Tocqueville Asset Management, the company had developed into an unquestionable success. But as we had grown, we had lost something essential—some of the spirit and proactiveness of our early days, the sense of ownership and initiative, the creativity and the client centeredness.

I yearned for the days when we were a compact, collegial team that could work efficiently and with the scrappy, energetic, even visionary drive of a young company eager to make a name for itself.

Of course we were making more money now, but the closeness of a small-team ambience and the daily fun that we had enjoyed in the earlier years had also been diminished. In my mind, the early adventure had been more satisfying than the current higher monetary rewards, and I missed it.

More critically, as we had lost an important part of what had made us attractive to both clients and new associates, I felt that our current growth might be endangering our future.

One day, I was discussing this unwelcome trend with Patsy Jaganath, who for many years had been diligently taking care of my main clients' patrimonial and administrative affairs and, in the process, had become very close to both my family and theirs. She argued that starting a smaller structure from scratch would be easier and smoother for clients than shrinking our existing institution to a desired size. Such a decision would go over better with my then partners, who took the culture I had created as a source of pride but preferred, in fact, to focus on more growth.

A secondary consideration also influenced my decision. Although my health was excellent, and I had no intention to abandon an activity that was my life passion, I had a duty to my longtime clients and to my own family to plan for the eventuality that something might happen to me someday. In other words, I needed a "family office" that would take care of my family and those of loyal friends if I was no longer there to do it myself. Borrowing a precept from our investment philosophy, I preferred to prepare for eventualities rather than try and predict the future.

If I were to start a separate firm independent from Tocqueville, excellent research would be essential to the successful management of my and our clients' fortunes, and I had in mind what I believed were our two best analysts: Allen Huang and Bogumil Baranowski. Both had started their careers at Tocqueville with me before taking responsibility for other firm projects, and I felt comfortable with their analyses and creativity.

From that point, things moved very fast. All three of my prospective new partners longed to become more entrepreneurial and immediately accepted the invitation to join the new project. My existing partners, on the other hand, proved less helpful in spite of my offers to cooperate in the future. Our departure from the firm I had created more than thirty years earlier was thus rather hurried. After a few weeks of literally camping, we signed a lease, arranged for strong custodial, compliance, and administrative partner firms, and obtained all the necessary regulatory authorizations in record time. We were now in business as Sicart Associates LLC, with four partners and two assistants, one on the fifty-fourth floor of the Carnegie Hall Tower in New York and the other one in Place de la Madeleine in Paris, which served as the hub for my European visits.

The Four Musketeers

Patsy, Allen, and Bogumil became the core of the new company. Besides our four-partner (including myself) brain trust, I took very little with me from Tocqueville's offices. One exception was a painting by the artist Leonid Sokov that I had bought from a Russian friend depicting Stalin embracing Marilyn Monroe. The artist's symbolic depiction of how the Eastern and Western civilizations perceived each other at the time of the Berlin Wall's fall was striking, and it fits even better in our new offices peopled by our multicultural team. Versions of that painting are now in various museums around the world.

The other treasure I took with me was the heavy desk that had belonged to my mentor, Christian Humann, who himself had received it from Ernie Borkland, a senior partner at Tucker Anthony, and which Bogumil now inherited. A symbolic fusion of tradition and change.

Once we opened our doors, we were able to find our stride quickly, with very little of the rocky adjustment period that accompanies most startup operations. In truth, we were a new company in name only, bolstered as we were by our strong working relationships both within ourselves and with our clients.

I recalled that, sometime after I had created Tocqueville Asset Management, I often worried that we had no formal organization chart or task assignments. Though problems all seemed to be taken care of somehow by someone, I had wondered if there might not be some organizing that we failed to implement. A former business schoolmate who had become a leading management consultant audited our small firm. He interviewed, at length, our six or seven professionals and concluded that we should not try to "change a winning team" and that the kinds of problems I was worrying about usually did not appear before a firm's size exceeded ten persons.

He also explained that the moment you start defining every task and responsibility, you are giving people an excuse to think, "This is not my job," and to skirt some responsibilities. That is when things begin to fall between the cracks—a pitfall I was determined to avoid, which is why I am leery of growth at any cost.

So far, we have felt no need to embark into tedious planning, and even today we have very little in the way of formal hierarchy or job titles. If a problem emerges, it is dealt with by the team—someone inevitably steps up. I don't feel the need to delegate responsibilities or manage anyone, for we are in sync, in synergy, a cohesive, smoothly running machine.

What Sets Sicart Associates Apart

I didn't found Sicart Associates merely to reproduce a smaller version of Tocqueville, but to carve out a niche that would distinguish us from the rest of the industry.

Wall Street is famous for its indefatigable drive toward growth—growth in the form of an ever-expanding suite of products, a bigger workforce, a larger clientele. Growth for growth's sake, growth at any cost. My goal was to create a more compact, leaner, more agile firm that would be unconcerned with any form of growth except that of the clients' funds.

Most firms nowadays are driven by their marketing departments. They are selling products, which in recent decades have burgeoned in number and complexity but without a concomitant increase in quality or profitability. (For the client, at least. These new product lines have been a tremendous boon to the firms' bottom lines.)

Basically, investment firms' marketing departments have hired a bevy of math geniuses to develop complex new products that promise higher returns or lower risk and sometimes both, which the marketing departments then tout to the public. This has created a new stream of revenue for the companies, which has only incentivized the marketing departments to go back to the math people and ask for more. With this mass-marketing approach, more and more employees of financial firms have become distanced from the clients and their needs and perhaps from investing fundamentals.

Of course, financial marketing departments and salespeople are not necessarily dishonest. But the fact is that, in finance especially, it is difficult to avoid potential conflicts of interest between a business and its clients. Many sources of such conflicts are regulated (order front-running, insider trading, etc.), but others are more subtle. At Sicart

Associates, we do not discount our services, but our clients never have to wonder where our interests lie.

The Way We Think about Investments

Bob Farrell, the legendary market strategist of Merrill Lynch for several decades, once published "10 Market Rules to Remember," which have since been reproduced many times. I cannot do better than to reproduce them again here:[2]

1. Markets tend to return to the mean over time.

2. Excesses in one direction will lead to an opposite excess in the other direction.

3. There are no new eras—excesses are never permanent.

4. Exponential rapidly rising or falling markets usually go further than you think, but they do not correct by going sideways.

5. The public buys the most at the top and the least at the bottom.

6. Fear and greed are stronger than long-term resolve.

7. Markets are strongest when they are broad and weakest when they narrow to a handful of blue-chip names.

8. Bear markets have three stages—sharp down, reflexive rebound, and a drawn-out fundamental downtrend.

---

2   Jonathan Burton, "Learn a lesson—before you get one," *MarketWatch*, June 11, 2008, https://www.marketwatch.com/story/ten-investing-rules-that-will-help-you-weather-this-stormy-market.

9. When all the experts and forecasts agree—something else is going to happen.

10. Bull markets are more fun than bear markets.

These seemingly common-sense rules may not seem very scientific, but they were the result of the daily observation of literally hundreds of economic, financial, and psychological indicators filtered through a wealth of historical knowledge.

At Tucker Anthony, I was lucky to work closely with Stanley Berge, who had achieved a popularity equal to Farrell's with major institutional investors. One of the secrets of those two star strategists, shared by very few others, was to recognize that no statistic correlates perfectly with the markets all the time. Many do so in most environments, but not always. So by keeping track of how many of their hundreds of favorite statistics flashed a buy or sell signal, they attained a superior *batting average* over time.

> **Making money over time is seldom a matter of yes or no; it is a matter of whether or not the odds are in your favor when you make a decision—often simply by avoiding the worst choices.**

Ned Davis, another iconic market student, once observed that aiming to be right was not the same as investing to make money. Making money over time is seldom a matter of yes or no; it is a matter of whether or not the odds are in your favor when you make a decision—often simply by avoiding the worst choices.

At Sicart, we operate on the assumption that trying to predict the future—particularly by timing markets or companies—is mostly a futile exercise for portfolio management. For example, it is less useful to guess where the price of oil will be in two or three years than to assess the consequences for companies, economies, and financial markets *if* that price should double or be cut in half.

Faced with a multitude of facts and data, most people develop quick opinions that, unfortunately, are subject to frequent change. Yet as Ernest Hemingway (no stranger to action) reportedly advised, *One should not confuse motion for action*. What is important is to develop convictions based on observation and analysis and then act decisively on them at (or around) the right time.

On the investment side, Sicart was founded on an ethos of "going against the herd." Just as we eschew growth for growth's sake, we stay above the fray of the relentless pursuit of short-term returns and studiously avoid the madness of crowds. In theory, a contrarian approach can be adopted by a larger wealth management company. But in practice, a small company like ours is better suited to contrarian value investing. When you become big, it's hard not to behave like a crowd. And the crowd is always wrong in the end because it is driven by bipolar instincts rather than by fundamental and rational analysis.

As contrarian value investors, we zero in on out-of-favor companies that have been marginalized by the market, usually because of temporary challenges rather than problems with the company itself. We are willing to look beyond these uncertainties as long as our analysis confirms the companies are strong enough to weather the storm and perform well in the future.

Typically, our picks have already underperformed long enough to have induced the majority of investors' capitulation. As a result, these stocks respond less and less to bad news, while negative market sentiment and media headlines lead to very few buy recommendations among Wall Street firms.

Certain types of businesses make attractive prospects:

1. Cyclical businesses that are experiencing transitory or anomalous setbacks, most likely due to their industry environment rather than management failures.

2. Underfollowed, unloved, misunderstood, and neglected businesses (whose outwardly "boring" nature obscures the long-term potential of some of their activities).

Historically, most of our profitable decisions have fallen into one of these categories. It is not that other analysts and investors cannot engage in this type of contrarian thinking, but we have longer time horizons and the patience to "give time the time," as a French president once said.

Our contrarian bias is nevertheless tempered by two caveats:

1. The umbrella theory: If everyone says that it is raining, it is dangerous to go out without an umbrella. The crowd is often right about the present or the near future, and the contrarian must be able to acknowledge but look beyond the near term.

2. The cockroach theory: There is never just *one* cockroach in the kitchen. Companies that fail because of tainted management practices seldom have just one temporary accident. Bad corporate culture is pervasive and leads to repeated problems.

Though strong values are harder to come by amid a highly efficient, algorithmically powered market, opportunities always exist. But when they are scarce, we hold cash and wait. Maintaining ample cash reserves is also an essential part of our strategy because it is psychologically harder to make the decision to invest in new opportunities when you have no cash to seize them. Another reason why our accounts typically hold more cash than most is that we usually accumulate new positions gradually—sometimes over a couple of years—to solidify our conclusions and test our value calculations.

Patience is more than just a virtue; it's a means of making our clients rich. Many analysts seldom look beyond companies' two-year outlooks. Consultants and boards of directors of major financial institutions increasingly demand that performance be measured and assessed over ever-shorter periods—the industry as a whole seems to grow more myopic as time goes by. But this preoccupation with the short term opens up opportunities for investors like us who are willing to investigate companies' prospects over longer horizons. While most analysts will only look at the next one, two, or—if they are very long term—three years, we tend to investigate scenarios five years out, as our goal is to build lasting wealth for multiple generations rather than earn immediate returns. And in this respect, we have found that it is better to *prepare* for eventualities than to try and predict them.

At first glance, contrarian value investing sounds simple. In practice, of course, it means sitting out irrationally exuberant rallies and gritting your teeth through major downturns, even doubling down on buys of a stock whose price is in the cellar. Our firm is like the stalwart vessel that cuts through the tempest calmly and coolly, knowing that it is all just part of the journey.

That's why it's important for clients to trust us. I recall one client who had become frustrated with my decision to eschew the hot tech stocks of the 1990s bubble as the indices climbed higher and higher, and everyone, it seemed, was getting rich. But you know how that story ended.

Years later, that client and I were having lunch when she said, "I knew the whole dot-com boom was crazy, but I often felt that you were not crazy enough—that you should have joined the fray. And now I know why I stayed with you."

An Unusable but Instructive Performance Record

There is one investment account which I managed or comanaged for more than forty years. I cannot claim that this represents my overall investment record, because it is only one among many accounts that I managed with different objectives and over different time periods. But it was by far the largest, the one with the longest audited record, and the one that I managed most freely.

I have not used its performance statistics for promotion, but I have regularly analyzed them to figure how and why the account performed as it did. Here are a few remarks that I have found useful.

In the first thirty-six years, from 1974 to 2010, the account recorded an average compound return of a little more than 1 percent per annum over that of the S&P 500 with dividends reinvested, to pick one popular benchmark.

Albert Einstein is reported to have remarked that compound interest was the eighth wonder of the world. My experience over the years seems to vindicate that observation. Just to give the reader an idea of how a mere 1 percent annual difference can mean over thirty-six years, a $10 million portfolio that grows at 12 percent per annum would be worth over $591 million thirty-six years later, while an equal account growing at only 11 percent per annum would become only about $428 million. In this example, a 1 percent annual difference in growth would add up to $163 million more in thirty-six years.

Our internal records show that the best period for this account was when the investment decisions were made by just two persons—myself and one comanager: first my partner and mentor Christian Humann, then my other partner Jean-Pierre Conreur. There may have been other factors, but I attribute the good performance of that account over its first thirty-six years at least in part to the fact that, most of the time, no more than a couple of people made the decisions. As I mentioned elsewhere, investing crowds tend to constitute the so-called dumb money that succumbs to herd instincts and tends to buy high and sell low.

The Elusive Safety in Diversification

The benefits and disadvantages of diversification are generally misunderstood by investors. For example, it appears that twenty-five stocks or so are enough to diminish the risk of an investment portfolio *if they operate in truly distinct activities*. But most institutions carry much more broadly diversified portfolios. That tends to lower short-term volatility but will usually produce herdlike (i.e., mediocre) results over the longer term.

Similarly, clients often feel that they would reduce their risk exposure by splitting their portfolio's management between several advisors. In fact, this kind of diversification may reduce volatility but not risk, because managers usually do not hold any money or assets and are only allowed to give buy-and-sell instructions. The assets are physically held by custodians, and the real risk is that one of these custodians might get into trouble. It therefore would make more sense to me to concentrate on a trusted manager while diversifying custodians.

Coming back to the account we were using as an illustration, the performance after 2010 and until mid-2016 was less compelling than during the first thirty-six years: a gain of less than half the almost 95 percent achieved by the S&P 500 index, for example. Of course, a gain is still a gain, and a few years with lesser progress may slow compounding but do not interrupt it.

Also, that latter period was one when momentum ruled, continuing the markets' recoveries that followed the financial crisis and Great Recession. Over fifty years, I have experienced several periods when the market was driven by momentum—the tendency for securities that have gone up to continue up until they no longer do. But I am still convinced that one of the reasons for that more difficult performance in later years is that this is when we decided to diversify the management of the account internally between several managers to proactively pacify clients who might feel that they had too many eggs in a single basket.

The Twenty-First Century Homme D'Affaires

Of course, trust involves a lot more than your client having confidence in your ability to know when and what to buy and sell. It is a matter of demonstrated integrity and strong relationships. The model I have personally tried to embody at Sicart Associates is that of the nineteenth-century homme d'affaires—an experienced generalist who manages the fortunes of families with great competence and loyalty. This individual can also deal with outside experts, such as lawyers and fiscalists, on behalf of his clients when needed because he understands the families' needs as well as (or sometimes better than) family members themselves.

Think of the homme d'affaires (or femme d'affaires, as the case

> **Trust involves a lot more than your client having confidence in your ability to know when and what to buy and sell. It is a matter of demonstrated integrity and strong relationships.**

may be) as a financial family doctor with a perspective that extends over multiple generations.

In this sense, my three partners and I are much more than just investment experts. We all have a keen grasp of how a family's finances and wealth-building strategy interfaces with matters related to taxation, wills and trusts, real estate, legal concerns, divorce and marriage, and other major life concerns. And we know how to communicate with the relevant professionals within each of these areas.

Patrimony management has grown in complexity since I first entered the business. Families themselves have become more complex and less traditionally structured in an era of blended families, second marriages, and cross-border relationships. The panoply of laws and regulations governing inheritances, taxation, and so forth would probably stretch from the sidewalk of Fifty-Seventh Street to the top of the Carnegie Hall building if you stacked them up. Local, state, federal, and extranational law and tax obligations interweave and crisscross in highly complicated, often opaque fashion, and for families with vast assets in multiple sectors and countries, the challenge of managing it all grows exponentially.

A team of experts is helpful for addressing specific areas, of course, but each expert is proficient only in his or her field. You also need a generalist who can coordinate all the moving parts and who understands the big picture at any given moment. Someone who can advise on crucial decisions that have a lifelong impact for you and your family. In that spirit we have positioned ourselves as hommes or femmes d'affaires: a nineteenth-century role resurrected for the unique concerns of twenty-first-century wealth management.

CHAPTER 8

The Sicart
Associates Family

JUST AS I have played the role of advisor to our clients and their children, and the role of father to two now fully grown children, I hope that I also have become a good counselor to my partners. For a long time now, I have had the privilege of working with these remarkable individuals, whom I handpicked as my founding partners among a group of very talented professionals. In terms of financial analysis or patrimony management, they are at least as skilled as I am and probably more so, so there is not much I do in the way of mentorship these days. One way I can still influence them is by instilling a lasting culture in our firm—a firm that embraces limited growth not as a curtailment but as a strength. A firm whose partners share my belief that we will be the best stewards of our clients' fortunes if we work in a congenial and caring atmosphere, where there are neither competing agendas nor internal politics—a balance that, as I have observed elsewhere, becomes hard to preserve once the team number grows too large.

The Importance of Being Different

One of the obvious but often overlooked theorems of good investment management is that if you want to be better than the majority, you first have to be different.

As I was preparing to start on my American adventure, a young professor of finance at HEC, my French business school, had also just decided to move to New York to manage his own small fortune on the stock market (his academic area of expertise) and, at the same time, to start a company to sell French espadrilles in America. As I said, he was only a few years older than me (just enough time to earn his American PhD) but brilliant enough to have impressed his students, of which I was one. We became friendly, but I then lost track of him for a few years.

The next I heard from him, his small fortune had melted in the market, and the espadrille business had closed. Although we had not been particularly close, this episode made me suspicious of conventional, theoretical education when compared with "street wisdom" or simple common sense.

This bias was reinforced by my years of association with Jean-Pierre Conreur before he lost a courageous fight against cancer.

When Tucker Anthony hired a new representative for its Paris office, which I supervised, the new representative mentioned that his previous firm employed a "super guy" as a liaison between their research department and their European offices. I met Jean-Pierre and immediately hired him as an analyst working directly with me.

Jean-Pierre had never studied past the French baccalaureate and thus spoke plainly, without the trendy vocabulary more typical of fresh MBAs. Although he was a fantastic idea generator, he often puzzled the people he came in contact with.

He found most of his investment ideas in the weekly list of stocks making new lows and prided himself on studying "roadkill." He usually started his presentations by listing all the things that were wrong with the companies he would recommend. Although he had passed his baccalaureate in the scientific section, he had a weird way of describing his companies' technologies that often made more traditional analysts roll their eyes.

I remember having to call the CEO of a company Jean-Pierre followed and, upon introducing myself, hearing, "Ah! That's the Frenchman who always calls only to ask us about our competitors …" He may have surprised his interlocutors, but he always caught their attention.

This first experience solidified my commitment to surround myself with colleagues who were somehow different. The makeup of Sicart Associates is a case in point. The four partners are all Americans (albeit some rather recent ones) but we all come from very different cultural backgrounds: French, Indian, Chinese, and Polish. This was not achieved to engineer some kind of diversity mandate: it is just that cultural backgrounds affect how you perceive events around you and react to them, which improves the versatility and reactivity of a team.

American culture is overwhelmingly binary: things are perceived as good or bad, positive or negative, black or white. This makes it very efficient and action oriented. Other cultures are more holistic and generally more nuanced. For example, many people around the world are reticent to flatly say "no"—sometimes out of sheer politeness, sometimes because they dislike direct confrontation. In a business negotiation, you might assume that your interlocutor not saying "no" means "yes," but that could sometimes be a costly misunderstanding.

At Sicart, I believe that cultural diversity and the proximity allowed by a small team gives us a hedge.

From Outside Auditor to Partner: Patsy Jaganath

In her previous job at the CPA firm where she worked before she came on board as an employee of Tocqueville Asset Management, Patsy was often entrusted with accompanying big clients during tax audits: she knew their cases well, and even though she knew nearly as much about taxes as the IRS agents themselves, she was unfailingly modest and consummately professional. While audits can sometimes be contentious, she always maintained a cool, even-tempered, amicable approach to the work. It was evident that this was a woman who was capable of any challenge you threw at her.

We first hired her at Tocqueville to work on various administrative and accounting activities. Then, when our COO fell sick, she took over his job (though not his official title) for a couple years. When Marcella Lang, my invaluable assistant for thirty-seven years, was set to retire, and as the legal and administrative tasks for my clients grew in complexity, I asked Patsy to join me to oversee the administrative part of the office. She handled that role with aplomb, just as she had handled everything we asked of her before.

She had already been filling that family specialist role when I started assembling the new team for Sicart Associates, so I said, "You've already been a de facto partner for me for so many years, so why don't you become an actual partner?"

By that time, she already knew more about the details of my clients' family affairs than I did, so she was indispensable. At Sicart Associates, she combines her skill in communicating with families with her professional expertise as an accountant and her experience navigating the vagaries of the tax codes (and not just the American tax code, but tax law in other countries). She is as well versed in the nuances of tax law and finance as any tax attorney, which is good, because a big part of her job involves interfacing with them. And she's always learning new things.

One quality I admire and appreciate about Patsy is that she is not shy in expressing her opinion or her will, and in fact she can be stubborn at times, though never in a confrontational way. But she also tends to be discreet, maybe a little reticent. Sometimes I wish she were a little more assertive, since her contribution to the discussion is unfailingly helpful, and in a small firm, there's no time to hold one's tongue; everything needs to be out on the table. But when she knows what's right for you, she will fight for it with unfailing loyalty. For client families, she constantly exhibits a compassion and proactiveness that never fails to elicit demonstrations of heartfelt gratitude.

IN PATSY'S WORDS

My own rise to partner at Sicart Associates was in many ways a happy accident, of the type that have illumined François's own career. Initially, I was working for a public accounting firm that did accounting and tax work for Tocqueville Asset Management, and after some time, François got to know me and offered me a job. In any event, I was spending so much time at their office that I felt like I was employed there already!

For a while, I handled various tasks, including accounting and COO responsibilities, but then François's long-time secretary was planning to retire and he asked if I would head a family office he was creating. I would be assuming some of her duties but also taking on new ones, so it was, in essence, an entirely new and as yet undefined position. I asked him to tell me about the job and he demurred, "Just try it out and see if you like it."

I was a little wary, especially because I had spent my entire career perfecting my expertise as an accountant, and I didn't want my skills to flag or a gap to emerge on my résumé. I knew my accounting. I knew how to do my balance sheet, my financial statements. I could speak to people about tax planning and minimizing their taxes, but I knew little about the administrative and family office side of the business.

My first day in the position I was basically tapping my pencil at my desk wondering what to do. There was no guide. There was no manual. There was nobody who preceded me to show me the role that I would come to play. François suggested I sit down with a lawyer with whom he had worked on behalf of the clients, who would be able to give me the background of the clients he represented. So I met with this lawyer, who started telling me about the families. And as I was listening and taking notes, all of a sudden, I understood that what we were really discussing were not "clients" or account numbers, but real life *stories*. The way to understand families was not through their balance sheet and portfolios but through the *narrative* that uniquely characterized each family.

That was a revelatory moment for me, and soon the nature of the job became clearer. Each family was a story unto itself, and Sicart Associates played a part in helping to write that story. Each day I delved more deeply into the stories of the families we worked with, putting faces and lives and legacies to the names and numbers on each account.

Most people's career trajectories proceed from general to specific as they cultivate expertise in certain niches. Mine has apparently followed a reverse path, from someone with a clear job description and title to one that progressively became more open and varied as I took on additional roles and developed new skills—a chameleonic ability to conform to the needs of the firm, or, more precisely, the needs of the clients.

Today, I don't have any titles on my business card, not even "partner," because my role is so varied. I act as a fiduciary to some of the long-term clients while making sure that the requisite tax returns are filed and taxes are paid, constantly looking for ways to minimize their tax burden. I liaise with lawyers who advise us on the financial and legal implications of changing jurisdictions or buying a new home, and I work to facilitate dialogue between parents and children about money matters, both in order to educate the children (who must also learn to preserve the family fortune) and to avoid conflicts between family members in the future. To build and strengthen relationships (between our firm and clients, and also between members of the families we work with) as the basis of patrimony management.

I listen, I try to solve problems, I try to answer questions. And if there's one I can't answer, I know where to go and find the right people who can answer it for me. Such is the role of the financial family doctor. Your general practitioner might not be an expert on every part of the body and every conceivable illness, but she's still the first person you see when your shoulder aches or you can't sleep. And if she doesn't have a cure then and there, she can speak to the relevant experts in order to solve the problem at hand. That, in essence, is my role—to fulfill many roles simultaneously.

That also requires dealing with the occasional crisis, which of course is another inevitable part of family life: crises are thankfully rare, but they happen. In one instance I had to arrange for an emergency medical transport across the Atlantic to New York, and then as the client was recovering in the hospital, I helped make sure he didn't incur massive tax liabilities or immigration problems owing to his unplanned, lengthy stay in the United States.

In another case, we had a client whose permanent residence was in the US and who earlier in life had inherited a large sum of money from his German grandmother. Though he had been assured by his attorney that all necessary paperwork had been filed and taxes paid, there had been some major oversights. The German officials put him and his sons on notice.

Unfortunately, that same attorney was having a personal crisis and was thus incapable of helping. The clock was ticking, and it fell on us to resolve the problem expeditiously. I had to mobilize a team, basically overnight, to handle this complex and rather arcane legal/financial/tax/estate problem.

As the deadline loomed, we sprang into action and went back through many years of documentation in order to complete the voluntary disclosure and tie up legal loose ends before the German finance ministry started cracking the whip. In this way, we could assure him and his sons that they could sleep soundly at night without worrying their assets would be seized.

The family comes to us for everything now, for matters financial as well as personal. We've earned their trust, hopefully for life. It's very rewarding to take a financial emergency like that and turn it into something more rewarding and satisfying. But that's just another day in the (family) office.

An Entrepreneur's Analyst: Allen Huang

Allen was referred to me by my cousin Russell Berman, a business lawyer who became acquainted with him when Allen was employed as the comptroller of a venture capital firm. My cousin, whose judgement I respect, had high praise for this young man and suggested I meet with him. That informal meeting quickly led to a job offer at Tocqueville Asset Management.

Allen fit in well there and was liked by everyone, but what won him admiration even more than his congenial nature was his bright mind, and he quickly established himself as a leading analyst. Years later, when I began to consider whom to recruit for my new company, Allen was at the top of the list. I always knew he was one of the best analysts at Tocqueville—maybe *the* best.

Allen's life story is compelling too. In fact, all four of us have followed a rather circuitous path (metaphorically as well as geographically) to end up where we are today, given that we are all expatriates who have made the United States our home.

Allen was born in China, in a time of byzantine economic controls and stringent travel restrictions: an era when opportunities for young people on the mainland were scant. The best career path for a bright, ambitious young man was to emigrate. Allen first went to Germany, where for a couple years he worked as a waiter in the restaurant owned by his aunt, but he was unable to obtain a visa to pursue further studies there. So he applied to study in the United States and won a scholarship to attend Denison University, after which he completed an MBA at Brigham Young University. Following business school, he secured his position at the venture capital firm where he was working when I first met him.

Allen is not as headstrong as Patsy or as loquacious as Bogumil, but he's good with people and can hold his own in the conversational department. This is particularly true when we do business in China, where the language barrier conveniently serves both of us—me because someone else assumes the burden of conversation and negotiation, and him because it prevents me from intervening all the time.

Allen possesses a strong business instinct that complements his analytical acumen well, and that makes him a vital part of our team. He looks at companies like an entrepreneur does. Consequently, he gets along very well with entrepreneurs and gives them advice freely. Many of the clients he has won are people who have built businesses from scratch and who recognize in Allen a man who grasps the way they think and who understands business as well as finance. His clients certainly appreciate that he can move adroitly in both fields.

Thanks to Allen, Sicart Associates has found a lucrative niche among well-to-do Chinese families whose fortunes are perhaps less vast than the megamillionaires who are regularly wooed by the likes of Barclays or HSBC but who nonetheless have assets to invest and want to find the right people to invest with. Our Asian clients may not have as much liquid cash as some of their wealthier counterparts, but they have significant wealth tied up in their companies, which may be valued anywhere from $100 million to a billion dollars. And when they eventually sell their shares, it will be for everyone's benefit that their money is managed by us.

IN ALLEN'S WORDS

I started with Tocqueville on the first trading day after 9/11, a rather inauspicious beginning to what would prove to be a fruitful career working alongside some fantastic, brilliant people.

My new role at Tocqueville was a significant departure from my previous area of focus, as it meant transitioning from corporate finance and private equity to working in the public equity markets, but François had faith that I was capable, and I was excited for a new challenge. At first, I worked mostly with Jean-Pierre Conreur and another partner as an analyst before eventually being promoted to portfolio manager. It wasn't until a few years into my tenure that François and I began working side by side. But that's when we learned that we made great collaborators.

We would take periodic business trips to China, where we made inroads into the growing Chinese market. During one such trip, we were courting the founder and CEO of a public company, and over lunch we talked about how we ran our respective businesses. The CEO, who was a millionaire many times over, advocated strict cost management and frugality in management. François agreed, saying that he took a similar approach in his business and loathed wasting money.

After lunch, as the CEO got in his car, a shabby old Volkswagen Santana, the Maserati the hotel sent to pick us up pulled up. The CEO said nothing but frowned at the apparent extravagance. François blushed and said, "Now, this is embarrassing!"

That was just one of many memorable experiences we enjoyed together in China, but that trip I remember especially because it was the first time François broached the idea of leaving Tocqueville to be a partner at Sicart Associates.

I like to think of us as a young company with an old company's depth of experience. In the industry today, most people have been in the business only ten or fifteen years. A senior executive might have twenty or thirty years to their name. It's rare you meet someone like François, who has worked on Wall Street for fifty years and has run his own company for forty of them. Someone who has lived through half a century of market ups and downs, regulatory changes, the rise and fall of business titans, the rise and fall of entire *industries* is uniquely positioned to manage private money for families, which is a different challenge than managing institutional money. Though the other partners and I haven't yet racked up that much experience, we've benefited greatly from François's tutelage.

And that's also how we think when it comes to managing clients' money: decades, not years. "Long-term" for a lot of investors means a year or two. We're on an entirely different timeline.

In the office, no one is making decisions unilaterally. We function as a team. And our strength derives from the small size of that team—not so big that you get bogged down in the proceduralism of a "committee," but not so small that you're a solitary analyst making decisions on your own, without the benefit of other perspectives to check and balance your own work.

Day to day, 70 to 80 percent of my work involves research. I work closely with Bogumil Baranowski, considering investment ideas, evaluating current investments, and studying prospective ones. François is not as involved in the decision-making but he still plays a role as we bounce ideas off him. In addition to research, I'm also the chief compliance officer for the firm. In a larger company this role would probably be fulfilled by a specialist. In a smaller company we wear more than one hat. But therein lies our strength: we don't need systems or hierarchy; things just get done.

That's the way things work around here, as François himself would tell you: we may have job titles, but ultimately they don't matter. We aren't four individuals so much as a cohesive unit that runs in flawless harmony.

The Renaissance Man: Bogumil Baranowski

There's no serendipitous story about how Bogumil and I crossed paths: he sent in his resume to Tocqueville Asset Management, and it landed on my desk. Then again, maybe that *was* the serendipity. A steady stream of applications was always flowing through our mailroom, and it was fortuitous for both of us that I even looked at his, especially since I was not even looking to hire someone at the time. But Bogumil's credentials and background caught my eye—a Polish guy and fluent French speaker who graduated from one of the best business schools in France.

Because he seemed much more interesting than the average candidate, I interviewed him and found him to be very articulate, thoughtful, and able to hold forth intelligently on a range of topics (in addition to being a skilled financial analyst). Bogumil, I would come to learn, devours an impressive number and variety of books, which contributes to his generalized intelligence.

After I hired him, he mostly worked alongside other partners in the firm to help them manage their portfolios, usually mutual funds and things like that, rapidly proving himself as a top analyst. On further reflection, Bogumil's early tenure at Tocqueville has certain parallels to my own start at Tucker Anthony. I, too, had been hired even though there wasn't an opening the company was trying to fill, but Christian Humann thought I ticked the right boxes, and so he created a position for me.

When I decided to leave Tocqueville, I knew Bogumil would be a strong addition to the new firm, not only as an analyst but as an important ingredient in the new culture, given his penchant for thinking different and his skills as an eloquent communicator who can speak and write as well in his third language (English) as in his first.

Bogumil excels in his role as representative of the company and is usually the one who speaks to various executives and professional groups on our behalf. Many of the investors he talks to work for technology companies and tend to be attracted to growth rather than value investing, but he is adept at understanding contrary viewpoints while making a convincing case for the strategy we employ.

I can't talk about Bogumil without mentioning some of his more colorful pastimes. He's an avid deep-sea diver as well as a licensed pilot. During the pandemic he moved with his fiancée (now his wife) to the Catskills, where they enjoy daily hikes beneath the regal red oaks and towering white pines. They got married in front of this type of landscape in a Zoom-like ceremony, which we all attended. After that, they took refuge from the COVID-19 pandemic in the Dominican Republic. Certainly not the typical lifestyle of a partner in a boutique Wall Street firm. But whether he's on land, on sea, or in the sky, Bogumil has the multidimensional vision, open mind, and tireless work ethic that we need, and we all thrive on his energy and eloquence. And he is an expert on picking locations with excellent internet connectivity!

IN BOGUMIL'S WORDS

It was about sixteen years ago. I was still a graduate school student in Paris, already curious and passionate about investing. By then, I had read every book on the topic I could find, especially on the value investing school of thought inspired by Warren Buffett, Charlie Munger, and Benjamin Graham. I had also become an avid reader of Mr. François Sicart's articles. At the time, an audacious dream was born. I wanted to come to New York City to work in the investment field.

It was perhaps an unlikely destination for someone born in Cold War Poland to two medical school students. I have witnessed both the centrally planned communist economy's failure and the successes and challenges of a free market economy during my life. I've seen vast fortunes being made and lost. I credit those formative years for my contrarian bone, which in many ways has helped me find opportunities and avoid trouble investing.

My dream started to come true after an unforgettable meeting with François, who would soon become my mentor, boss, and eventually partner. I had one thousand questions racing through my head the morning we met. Most of all, I eagerly wanted to know more about the ways to *avoid losing* money rather than *making* it, since, as I learned later, the latter takes care of itself, and the former can get you in real trouble. In time, I would receive the answers to all my questions, and more, under François's tutelage. In fact, without his generosity, kindness, and wisdom, I wouldn't be where I am today.

In many ways, our fortunate encounter in Paris, days before Christmas in 2004, had significant parallels with him meeting his own mentor, boss, and partner, Mr. Christian Humann. They met back in 1969, one-third of a century earlier, days after one of the biggest blizzards New York City had ever seen forced the closure of the New York Stock Exchange, the first time such a closure happened due to weather.

Though I never had a chance to meet Mr. Humann, I feel I have had the pleasure of getting to know him through stories. And I have the honor of sitting at his very desk that François later used and then so generously allowed me to enjoy these last few years.

That's the kind of longevity and endurance one could only hope for in the investment profession. I am privileged to benefit from the intellectual heritage that dates back many generations, possibly centuries, a legacy of loyal, dutiful keepers of family fortunes for which we continue to care.

Our first conversation was just the beginning of my education as a contrarian investor. With François's guidance, I soon realized that there is so much more to investing than just buying stocks that go up and avoiding those that could go down. He introduced me to the world of family fortune investing. My investment horizon expanded from years to decades and generations. He showed me how his investment decisions have helped keep and grow a number of family fortunes over half a century.

In today's world of passive index investing, high-frequency trading, and transitory investment fads, François has been an even-keeled voice shaping my investment philosophy and helping me see where the true North Star can be found. He has never stopped pointing out constant challenges that family fortunes face year after year and opportunities available to those who care to look and dare to go against the crowd.

Though it was my comfort with numbers and curiosity about history that first got me into investing, it was the people who have kept me inspired, intrigued, and engaged over the years. It was François who always reminded me of the families and individuals behind the portfolios we manage. This understanding of our profession helped me improve my investment decisions and allowed me to serve our clients better.

Over the years, I built on my European education at the leading universities in Paris, Brussels, Warsaw, and with my own curiosity and my New York City experience, I shaped my investment approach. I wrote two investment books: *Outsmarting the Crowd* and *Money, Life, Family*. Both are inspired by what I have learned managing family fortunes over the long run. I also enjoyed many opportunities to give talks about family investing from the West Coast to the East Coast, including a TEDx talk in California, and around Europe from the sunny Canary Islands to the snow-covered Swiss Alps. My writing and speaking allowed me to grow a wide following in the US and overseas and helped me attract a new generation of clients, including those blessed with family inheritance, first-generation wealth creators, entrepreneurs, and tech professionals.

Though sixteen years have passed since our first conversation, I still continue to learn from François. I greatly admire how he built two prosperous businesses, thanks in large part to his gift for attracting diverse, talented, curious people to work with and wonderful clients to serve. With that in mind, he has created enduring, lifelong relationships built on loyalty and trust. That's the kind of longevity that's never been more important even as it has become increasingly rare in our profession.

I'm looking forward to many more successful decades of our investment practice. I trust that François's wisdom, experience, and legacy will continue to shape the family fortunes we care for and the next generations of investment advisors.

CHAPTER 9

Past, Present, and Future: Seizing Opportunities

IN MY YOUTH I had many dreams, as do young people everywhere. Now, decades later, I reflect with amusement on some of them. My initial ambition was to invent another penicillin. But I failed my first biology exam and shifted into accounting instead, figuring that if I couldn't eradicate the world of some terrible disease, at least I could eradicate some messy balance sheets. As it turned out, even though I taught it for two years to candidates in the French equivalent of the CPA exam, I wasn't passionate about accounting

> Taking the long view is part of being a successful investor, as it is with any occupation in life. But it must be used with an opportunistic awareness to recognize opportunities when they present themselves and to seize them swiftly.

occasion when he asked: "You liked XYZ when we bought the shares at one hundred dollars; do you still like it?" I explained why we did, and he then only asked: "It is now seventy dollars. How come we have not bought more?"

As I said, H. had an innate sense of value, but one of his greatest strengths was to judge people, and once he had decided he had the best—whether in art selection or in financial investments—he let his selected lieutenants do their thing. To me, the ability to do this is a sure mark of self-confidence, of judgement, and thus, in the end, of *character*.

E. was another example of great client. He was a second-generation fortune inheritor with an overwhelming sense of responsibility to preserve the family fortune and pass it along to future generations.

For a number of years, he had been a colleague in the financial industry and had managed his own investments quite well. We had often compared notes and shared ideas but, as the financial environment changed and the investment universe became more global, he decided to entrust me with the management of his portfolios and to concentrate (often with my advice) on more specifically patrimonial and generational matters. Yet, due to his experience and continued interest in finance, he was much more hands-on than H., for example.

More than once we disagreed but, though E. could be stubborn like my father, he also exhibited an unfailing intellectual honesty. That meant that *upon thinking further,* he was occasionally ready to admit that his interlocutor had been right.

This, of course, happened in matters of finance, but it was more striking on patrimonial matters. More than once, on the stewardship of his family rather than on technical or tax options, we disagreed. The choice was obviously his since it was his family. But often, after several days of deep solitary reflection, he would announce that he had reached the best decision—whether it was an original idea or one derived from my suggestions. Interestingly, E. did not, like many inheritors, surround himself with a multitude of advisors on all aspects of patrimony management. He trusted his own judgement on people and avoided the confusion of too many opinions that confuse rather than focus the mind.

Again, *character* manifested itself as a unique combination of strong self-confidence and intellectual modesty.

Learning, Doing, Teaching

Until his death in 2013, Leon Danco was one of the nation's top experts in advising family firms, and he built a very successful business around this niche. I had the fortune of meeting him one day, introduced by a mutual friend of ours. It was around the time I created Tocqueville Asset Management, when I was getting started on my entrepreneurial journey just as he was in the waning years of his. When I asked how he planned to spend his retirement, he answered, "Meeting people like you." He kept me all day and never charged me for a uniquely enlightening exchange.

The lessons Leon espoused, and which he wrote about in his book *Beyond Survival: A Guide for Business Owners and Their Families*, have greatly influenced me. One of his ideas involves dividing one's life into three periods of "learning years," "doing years," and "teaching years." The learning years span the first quarter century or so, when we are honing skills, acquiring knowledge, and learning how to think and to navigate the world—the mental, intellectual, and emotional development that prepares us for the busy phase of our "doing years," which is our most productive epoch, the prime of our careers that lasts until age fifty or sixty. At that time we transition into the "teaching years," family is also financially helping a number of charities, but what has impressed me most is the *immaterial* legacy that my wife, Régine, who recently passed away, quietly built over the years. Upon her passing, I received an amazing number of testimonies from younger people telling me how important she had been in their lives, both as a model and as a mentor.

As I reflect about this, I can't help becoming envious at how many people Régine influenced through her work and friendships. In our modern societies, success is often measured in monetary terms, sometimes in terms of power and, more recently, to close the circle, in terms of one's public recognition or branding, which itself can bring a degree of power or fortune. But, in terms of one's legacy, I am increasingly convinced that being the richest man in the cemetery or having once been powerful does not beat having positively influenced many lives, as Régine so obviously did. I, too, hope that I am leaving a legacy that can be measured by how many individual lives I have touched for the better.